LICENSING ART & DESIGN

By
Caryn R. Leland

ALLWORTH PRESS, NEW YORK

Published by Allworth Press, an imprint of Allworth Communications, Inc., 10 East 23rd Street, New York, New York 10010.

Distributor to the trade in the United States and Canada: North Light Books, an imprint of F&W Publications, Inc., 1507 Dana Avenue, Cincinnati, Ohio 45207. To order additional copies of this book, call toll-free (800) 289-0963.

Book Design by Douglas Design Associates, New York, New York.

Library of Congress Catalog Card Number: 89-80743

ISBN: O-927629-04-6

This book is designed to provide accurate and authoritative information with respect to the subject matter covered. It is sold with the understanding that the publisher and author are not engaged in rendering legal or other professional services. If legal advice or other expert assistance is required, the services of a competent attorney or professional person should be sought. While every attempt is made to provide accurate information, the author or publisher cannot be held accountable for errors or omissions.

Table of Contents

W hether you are a graphic designer with an idea for ceramic collectibles, an architect with plans to design exclusive furniture pieces, or an illustrator who envisions a new line of watches with limited edition watchface designs, no doubt you have wondered how to transform these ideas and concepts into a financially successful endeavor. These aspirations oftentimes are not realized because design professionals do not know how to begin the process or how to ask the pertinent questions—all because they lack an understanding of the fundamental means by which this process can be achieved. *Licensing Art & Design* introduces the reader to licensing—the customary method by which this transformation can be accomplished.

The book presents an overview of the business and legal aspects of licensing and takes the reader step by step through the licensing process, highlighting problem areas and offering practical solutions where possible. Marketing considerations, when relevant, are discussed.

Chapter 1 places licensing in a contemporary economic context and provides an introduction to the basic elements of licensing to familiarize the reader with these concepts.

Chapter 2 focuses on the rights of creators of art works and designs. It introduces the reader to the fundamental legal principles of the "law of ideas," and copyright, patent, and trademark laws—the bedrock of licensing arrangements—and reviews the interrelationship of these laws and the protections they offer.

Chapter 3 suggests ways for the design professional to safeguard and secure rights in and to ideas and concepts in the pre-licensing stage. The importance of using nondisclosure and confidentiality agreements to prevent loss of rights in original ideas and materials prior to securing a contract is explained. The chapter reviews the major provisions that these agreements should cover. A suggested "Model Nondisclosure Agreement" is included at the end of the chapter.

The most important document in the relationship between the creator of a work and the purchaser of the rights to market the work is the licensing agreement. To understand licensing contracts and to master the intricacies of such arrangements, a working knowledge of the legal principles of contract law and a familiarity with the salient points of a typical licensing agreement are essential.

Chapter 4, the heart of the book, addresses these concerns. It contains a licensing agreement reproduced in full, and explains each provision against a backdrop of a simulated licensing deal. It evaluates the legal, business, and practical implications of each of the terms and conditions.

Chapter 5 contains a suggested "Model Long Form Licensing Agreement" and a suggested "Model Short Form Licensing Agreement." These model agreements are designed to be used (with appropriate modifications) by artists and designers as proposed licensing agreements. A "Checklist for Negotiating Licensing Agreements," which serves as a ready summary of the key points of a licensing arrangement, appears at the end of the chapter.

Chapter 6 considers the advisability of designers and artists hiring licensing agents and representatives to secure licensing deals. It evaluates the reasons for and against doing so. A suggested "Model Agency Agreement" is provided at the end of the chapter.

When using this book, the designer or artist should remember that no legal or business guide can be a substitute for solid, up-to-date advice provided by a professional with expertise in the subjects impacting on the particular field in which information is sought. Licensing is no exception.

Chapter 1

Introduction to Licensing

L icensing is about selling certain rights to images. More particularly it is about selling these rights for specific purposes or for particular applications. Character licensing—that is, the use of Mickey Mouse and Donald Duck, or Big Bird, Garfield, or Pee-wee Herman to promote the sale of toys, apparel, school supplies, greeting cards, to name just a very few of the myriad of products sold bearing these images—represents one large aspect of licensing.

Another aspect of licensing—the commercial exploitation of fine and graphic visual art images for use on textiles, wall coverings, apparel, greeting cards, giftwrap, household accessories, towels, sheets, china and ceramics, paper goods, posters, and stationery—is the focus of this book. The ways in which these images can be licensed is limited only by the breadth of one's imagination and creative powers. This area constitutes almost 10 percent of all licensing and is responsible for producing over $5 billion in retail sales annually and generating royalty income for artists and designers in the amount of $75-100 million.

More than ever, increasing numbers of designers and artists are becoming involved in licensing. Numerous private companies organize licensing expositions where those who create the designs and images have an opportunity to introduce their work to the companies that license it (and sometimes purchase it outright). Sponsors of these expositions include the New York-based Licensing Industry Merchandisers' Association (LIMA), 350 Fifth Avenue, New York, New York 10118, (212) 244-1944, and George Little Management, Inc., 2 Park Avenue, New York, New York 10016, (212) 686-6070. Both groups charge fees for attending these shows and LIMA has a formal membership program. In addition to promoting licensing shows, companies like these publish newsletters and provide other helpful information.

Publications like *Advertising Age, Stores, Forbes, Business Week, The Wall Street Journal,* and the business sections of national newspapers should be perused from time to time to keep abreast of developments. Simply frequenting the shops and stores which sell the products on which designers and artists hope to see their work is also a good way to monitor and perhaps anticipate trends. The "Resources for Artists and Designers" included in the Appendices lists other important shows, fairs, trade organizations, and publications.

The License Defined and Described

A *license* is an agreement for the transfer or grant of rights in a work by the owner of those rights to another. The vocabulary of licensing consists of these essential terms: the owner of the image is known as the *licensor;* the image is referred to as the *licensed property,* and the recipient of the grant of rights is called the *licensee.* The *grant* of the license describes the terms for the use of the image and includes such other points as the territory and length of time the license is effective. Unlike an outright sale of work, a license does not transfer title to the physical work.

Characteristically, a licensing agreement gives the licensee the right to use the licensed property (for example, a design) for a specific purpose (on wallpaper) for a limited time (two years) in a specified territory (United States). In exchange, the licensee customarily pays a *royalty* to the licensor.

A royalty is usually a percentage of the proceeds received from the sale of the licensed product. It can be based on the selling price (either wholesale or retail), less certain production or selling expenses. A royalty can also be based on a fixed dollar amount per licensed product sold. In addition, a licensing agreement can require the licensee to pay a nonrefundable *advance* against royalties. An advance is an amount of money paid to the licensor in anticipation of royalties before the licensed product is sold.

A license of a design can be *exclusive* to a licensee, meaning the licensee is given the exclusive right to market the licensed property, or *nonexclusive*, meaning, for example, that other licensees have the same or overlapping rights with regard to the licensed property. Refer to chapter 4 for an in-depth explanation of these terms and the structuring of licensing arrangements.

The source of licensing is the ownership of the rights of copyright, trademark, and patent. A simple way to look at licensing is to view the ownership of these rights collectively as a pie, with ownership thereof bestowing upon the artist or designer the sole right to divide the pie as he or she determines. The allocation and distribution of the slices constitutes the essence of licensing. The skillful carving of the pie—the selling of one image for different applications—is the key to successful licensing.

The Need for a Written Agreement

Why have a written contract? Practical considerations abound for having written contracts. First, it is easy to mistake preliminary discussions with a company's representative as a firm offer to undertake a licensing venture. Though the initial discussions can serve as the basis for the eventual written contract, generally these types of discussions lack details sufficient to constitute a binding agreement.

Second, in addition to setting forth each party's respective rights and obligations, a written agreement can help reduce discord and encourage cooperation. It can serve as a ready reference for settling disputes concerning the intent of the parties at the time the agreement was signed. Should a problem arise which necessitates judicial intervention, the contract provides a most reliable and convincing form of evidence.

Third, licensing art and design involves esoteric areas of the law. It also calls into play sophisticated negotiating and bargaining skills which most artists and designers unfortunately do not possess. First-time licensors who most need professional advice usually do not seek it, either because they are not aware of the potential pitfalls which lie ahead, or if they are, because they cannot afford to retain an attorney at the initial stage. Without a rudimentary understanding of the basic issues involved in licensing, the artist is distinctly disadvantaged. Reference to an agreement, like the sample form, can help focus the preliminary discussions and improve the designer's bargaining position.

Fourth, in what is characterized in contract law as the "Battle of the Forms," i.e., the negotiation process determining whose version of the agreement is used, an artist's offering his or her version first increases the chances of the artist's or designer's terms being accepted. Having a licensing agreement to offer the potential licensee enhances the bargaining process for the designer by placing the designer in a stronger position psychologically. It fosters respect from business people who are comfortable with and expect to be presented with contracts for review.

Using the designer's version (presumably developed beforehand with a lawyer) can reduce legal expenses for the designer, since the designer's attorney already knows the contents of their agreement and does not have to expend time reviewing the licensee's. The lawyer's time can be expended more efficiently by honing in on fewer points to reach an understanding.

Chapter 2

Copyrights, Trademarks, and Patents Distinguished

Ownership of the rights of copyright, trademark, and patent in and to works created by artists and designers gives them the right to control and exploit their work commercially. For with ownership comes the legal right to prevent others from using and exploiting a work without permission. Through the skillful sale of these rights under licensing arrangements, creators in the visual arts and design fields can generate substantial income. Yet before licensing agreements are contemplated, the artist or designer should acquire a basic understanding of the laws governing licensing. Successful negotiation requires a knowledge of the scope and limits of these rights, sometimes referred to as "intellectual property" rights.

Copyrights, trademarks, and patents confer overlapping rights and protection. However, each can function independently of the other. Thus a product can be the subject of one or more forms of protection. For example, a desk lamp can be protected by a copyright (the lamp as a work of sculptural art), by a utility patent (the unique armature assembly), by a design patent (the aesthetic appearance of the lamp), and by a trademark (the unique appearance of the lamp as a symbol of the manufacturer's products). Whether multiple protections are sought depends on various considerations. As discussed in this chapter, one form of protection may be more suitable for a particular work or for the needs of one creator than another.

Copyrights

The Copyright Law, which is governed exclusively by federal law, protects the created work at the point that the idea for the work is fixed in a tangible medium of expression. A work is "fixed in a tangible medium of expression" when its embodiment is "sufficiently permanent or stable to be perceived, reproduced, or otherwise communicated for a period of more than transitory duration." Copyright ownership is the source of all rights of usage in and to a work. The basic term of a copyright is the life of the author plus 50 years.

For a work to be copyrightable, three elements must be satisfied. First, the work must be fixed in a tangible form from which it can be reproduced. Second, it must be the result of original independent authorship (though the entire work need not be original; it can be based on prior copyrighted or uncopyrighted material). Third, there must be a minimal element of creativity present.

The scope of copyright is limited. Copyright protects only the expression of an idea, not the idea or concept itself. Ownership of the copyright in a work does not give the author ownership of the underlying idea. This principle stems from the traditional belief in and encouragement of the free flow of ideas. Granting an exclusive right to an idea to an individual, at the exclusion of all others, weakens rather than strengthens society. Names, titles, trademarks, short phrases, and slogans are not copyrightable since they are deemed to lack the minimum amount of original authorship necessary for copyright.

Copyrights are not available for utilitarian or functional objects, that is, "useful articles." The design of a useful article can be registerable, however, but only if and to the extent that the design incorporates artwork that can be identified separately and can exist independently from the utilitarian aspects of the article. For example, a dining room chair itself is not copyrightable; however, its aesthetic sculptural elements may be. Design patent registration (see discussion which follows) may afford the necessary protection for the design of the chair. Designers should note that artwork on labels, packaging, and advertising for articles is copyrightable to the extent that the artwork satisfies the twin tests of separateness and independence.

Copyright laws apply to all types of published and unpublished works of authorship, including: literary works (books, magazines, and manuscripts), works of the performing arts (musical works, choreographic works, and motion pictures), and works of visual arts. Works of visual arts consist of pictorial, graphic, and sculptural works, and include two-dimensional and three-dimensional works of fine, graphic, and applied art (such as photographs, prints and other art reproductions, maps, globes, charts, diagrams, models, and architectural plans).

Ownership of the copyright in a work is separate from ownership of the work. This means that copyright in and to a work can be sold or disposed of separately from the work itself. For example, an illustrator can retain ownership of the original art for the cover of a record album and sell only the right to reproduce the work on the cover. And, if not limited by the terms of this sale, the illustrator can also sell the art to others for additional uses, for example, on posters.

The ownership of a copyright vests the author with five exclusive rights:

1) to reproduce the copyrighted work in copies;

2) to prepare derivative works that are based upon the copyrighted work;

3) to distribute copies of the copyrighted work to the public by sale or other transfer of ownership, or by rental, lease, or lending;

4) to perform the copyrighted work publicly in the case of literary, musical, dramatic and choreographic works, pantomimes, and motion pictures and other audiovisual works;

5) to display the copyrighted work publicly in the case of literary, musical, dramatic and choreographic works, pantomimes, and pictorial, graphic, or sculptural works, including the individual images of a motion picture or other audiovisual work.

These exclusive rights of copyright are divisible, meaning that each right can be divided and disposed of separately without jeopardizing or lessening the value of the remaining rights. The holder of the exclusive rights to a particular right of copyright is the owner of the copyright for that right and can develop and use the right as he or she sees fit. The typical way of disposing of these rights is through licensing arrangements which are discussed at length in chapter 4.

The exercise of any of the exclusive rights of copyright without the authorization of the owner constitutes copyright infringement. To succeed in an action for infringement of a copyrighted work, the plaintiff has to prove "access to the work" and "substantial similarity." Copyright infringement actions can be brought only in federal court. A plaintiff can seek an injunction against continuing and future infringements and either compensatory damages (the infringer's profits and the actual damages suffered by the owner) or statutory damages (which are awarded at the court's discretion and range from $500 to $20,000 per infringement, with a $100,000 maximum for willful infringement, and $200 minimum for innocent infringement).

A work is protected by the copyright laws the moment it is created in a tangible form. Though the artist is not required by law to register the work or place his or her copyright notice on the work before it is published, it is recommended that the artist safeguard the copyright by doing so. The notice literally advises the viewer that the creator claims rights in the work and permission must be obtained prior to any use.

From January 1, 1978, until March 1, 1989, the copyright law required artists to place their copyright notice in the proper statutory form on all their works when published or risk losing copyright unless the artist acts quickly enough and takes specific steps to correct the situation. "Publication" for purposes of the copyright law means "the distribution of copies...of a work to the public by sale or other transfer of ownership, or by rental, lease, or lending. The offering to distribute copies...to a group of persons for purposes of further distribution, public performance, or public display, constitutes publication."

On March 1, 1989, the Berne Implementation Act of 1988 became effective. The passage of this act enabled the United States to join the Berne Convention (an international agreement governing copyright law). Membership in the Berne Convention eliminated the former statutory requirement for the placement of copyright notice on a work as a condition of protecting the copyright.

Although the notice requirement is no longer mandated, better practice dictates that notice be used to signal the creator's rights in a work and to cut off potential claims of innocent infringements of the work. From a practical standpoint, from March 1, 1989, on, anyone seeking to use published, copyrightable material should assume that the work is protected by copyright even though no notice appears. Thus, before any such work is used, the appropriate permission should be obtained.

The proper statutory form of copyright notice is: the symbol ©, or the word "copyright," or "copr."; the name of the copyright "owner" (note that the owner may not be the author but a transferee), or an abbreviation by which the name can be recognized, or a pseudonym by which the owner is known; and the year of first publication (this may be omitted on greeting cards, postcards, stationery, jewelry, dolls, toys, and useful articles).

Each licensing agreement should require that the licensee place the licensor's statutory copyright on the licensed products and on all packaging, advertising, and promotional materials as well. The license should also require the licensee to submit samples of these materials prior to distribution to insure that the notice requirements have been complied with.

Because copyright protection exists from the moment the

author has fixed the work in tangible form, registration of the copyright is not required as a condition of copyright ownership. However, registration is recommended. The application for registration should be filed as soon as possible after the creation of the design. Registration within three months after publication preserves certain rights and allows the owner to recover statutory damages and attorneys' fees if there is an infringement of the work.

Registration is a rather simple process that requires the submission of a registration form, a deposit of the work for which copyright is sought, and payment of the statutory fee of ten dollars, though there is a proposal pending to increase this fee to twenty dollars. To save on registration fees, groups of unpublished works (in the form of a "collection") can be registered under one application with one application fee. A copyright can be registered at any time during the term of the copyright by filing the appropriate copyright registration form (Form VA for visual arts works, Form TX for nondramatic literary works, and Form PA for works of the performing arts). The application forms for copyright registration can be obtained free of charge by writing to the Copyright Office, Library of Congress, Washington, D. C. 20559. The Hotline Number for Forms and Circulars is (202) 707-9100, and the Public Information Number is (202) 479-0700.

The Copyright Office also publishes a series of helpful informational circulars, including, "The Nuts and Bolts of Copyright," "Highlights of the New Copyright Law," "New Registration Procedures," and "Deposit Requirements for Registration of Claims to Copyright in Visual Arts Material." These are available at no charge and can be obtained by writing the Copyright Office at the above address.

A work should be registered for a number of reasons. Registration is a prerequisite to bringing a lawsuit for infringement of works created prior to March 1, 1989, and also for works of United States origin created after March 1, 1989. Registration within three months after the work's first publication allows the plaintiff to recover attorneys' fees and to use an easier method to establish monetary loss caused by the infringement, known as "special" statutory damages. Issuance of a copyright registration by the United States Copyright Office gives a statutory presumption as to the validity of the copyright and provides evidence to help establish the existence of a particular work and its date of creation.

There are circumstances when the creator of a work automatically will not own the right to the copyright. This can arise when the work produced is considered to be a "work made for hire." The determination of whether a work is a work made for hire is important for creators of artwork as well as for design firms or advertising agencies which order, supervise, or purchase artwork. A work made for hire consists either of a work prepared by an employee within the scope of his or her employment or certain work (but not all types of work) ordered or commissioned, if both parties sign a written agreement stating that the work is made for hire. If a work is a work made for hire, the employer or person for whom the work is prepared is treated automatically by the copyright law as the creator of the work. It is this person, and not the artist, who is entitled to seek copyright registration therein, and it is this person who has the legal right to decide how to exploit the work.

Frequently companies require creators of work who provide artwork under freelance or commission arrangements to sign away all rights to the work. This can be achieved through the use of contracts by placing forfeiture conditions on purchase orders and invoices or by using work-for-hire clauses as a condition for payment. For example, a restrictive endorsement written on the back of a check may state that the cashing of the check constitutes an acceptance that the work (or future works, if the provision is so written) is a work made for hire. Some companies require artists and designers to sign a blanket work-for-hire agreement that requires the artist to sign away all rights in a particular work and in all future work in exchange for a single fee. "All rights," or "Work for hire," should be viewed as warning flags if either appears in a contract.

Another instance when the creator of a work can find his or her work used by another without violating the creator's copyright is when the use by another is claimed to be "fair use." The doctrine of "fair use" is recognized by the copyright law. When applicable, it permits a lawful use of copyrighted work without the owner's consent. Fair use serves as a defense to an action for copyright infringement when the alleged infringer claims that the unauthorized use of the owner's copyrighted work is fair and lawful rather than an infringement of copyright law. Legally recognized examples of fair use include: use of a copyrighted work for criticism, comment, parody, satire, news reporting, teaching, scholarship, and research.

The doctrine remains broad and its broadness defies easy definition. Whether a particular use constitutes a fair use is determined on a case-by-case basis. Where the use is for commercial gain and detrimental to the commercial viability of the copyright owner's work, a fair use defense is less likely to be upheld. As the work of designers and artists is frequently subject to pirating and appropriation through computer scanning and graphic manipulation, copyright owners should diligently police their work and seek professional assistance to determine if an unauthorized use is an actionable infringement.

Work which is in the public domain is not subject to copyright protection. Visual images enter the public domain in several ways: one, the image is not copyrightable; two, copyright was lost through a failure to adhere to the law's requirements; or three, the copyright expired. Anyone, including the artist or designer, may use and copy public domain work freely without risk of violating the copyright laws. Although free to use public domain works in part or in their entirety, those who do so must remember that copyright is not available for the resultant work, and, as a consequence, anyone would be free to use and copy the work. The one exception to this situation is that the addition of original material to public domain work can qualify the new work for copyright protection. However, the protection only will cover the "new" elements of the work.

Patents

The source of patents is also federal law. The grant of a United States patent confers upon the inventor, known as the "Patentee," an exclusive right to make or sell the invention or design throughout the United States during the term of the patent. It is an exclusive, "monopolistic" grant. The patentee can prevent individuals from knowingly copying the patent or even innocently infringing it.

Patents are of three types. The first, "Utility Patents," are granted for any new and useful machine, process, manufacture, and composition of matter, or any new and useful improvement thereof. The second, "Design Patents," hold the most interest for persons active in the visual arts and design fields. A design patent is granted for any new, original, and ornamental design for an article of manufacture. It offers a means to protect the "look" or "configuration" of a particular article or its packaging when copyright is not available. To satisfy the ornamental requirement, the design must be aesthetically pleasing and cannot be solely or primarily dictated by functional or mechanical considerations. The third type of patent, "Plant Patents," are granted for the invention or discovery and asexual reproduction of a distinct and new variety of plant.

The term of the patent varies according to type: seventeen years for a utility patent, fourteen for a design patent, and an indeterminate time for plant patents. Like copyrights, patents are exclusively federal, but unlike copyrights, a patent does not exist the moment a work is created; it must be applied for from the federal government and granted.

A patent application is filed with the Patent and Trademark Office, together with the required statutory filing fee (a minimum of $340 for utility patents, $140 for design patents—both fees are reduced by half if the applicant is a sole or independent inventor). The application is reviewed, and, if all the requirements are satisfied, a patent will be issued. During the time the patent application is under consideration by the Patent and Trademark Office, the subject of the application should be marked "patent pending." Upon issuance of the patent, this notice must be replaced with the actual patent number, for example: "U.S. Patent No. 5,0015,089."

The preparation, filing, and application costs incurred in obtaining a patent can be substantial, easily exceeding several thousand dollars. The process is lengthy—years may pass before the patent is obtained. However costly and time-consuming, the grant of an exclusive monopoly for the license of the patent and the expected royalties, in the appropriate case, may justify the expense. This is an area of licensing that requires the expert advice of individuals schooled in patent law.

Inventors and designers should act carefully so as not to

risk loss of the idea by premature disclosures to individuals who have not agreed to maintain secrecy. See the discussion of the use of nondisclosure agreements to maintain secrecy in chapter 3.

Patent owners can sue infringers for injunctive relief and for damages in an amount "adequate to compensate for the infringement but in no event less than a reasonable royalty for the use made of the invention by the infringer, together with interest and costs." The trial court has the discretion to award treble damages in exceptional cases and to award attorneys' fees to the prevailing party.

Trademarks

Generally a trademark or other mark is a symbol adopted and used by a person or company to identify the source of goods and services and to distinguish them from the goods and services of another. A trademark can consist of: letters, words, symbols, acronyms, monograms, phrases, numerals, abbreviations, slogans, titles, logos, character or personality images, pictures, labels, shapes, packages, and configurations of goods or combinations thereof which identify goods and distinguish them from those manufactured or sold by others.

Graphic designers and related freelancers probably are most familiar with trademarks as company logos or as a part of distinctive packaging systems designed to symbolize or enhance corporate identity. The work utilized in these projects is sold outright and fees are calculated on the basis of usage and reproduction rights purchased. Ordinarily these types of arrangements are not the subject of licensing arrangements. There are instances, however, when a designer may agree to receive a smaller design fee in exchange for receiving additional payments based on a percentage of sales from the products bearing the particular logo or incorporating the packaging design. This type of arrangement would fall under the category of licensing.

The customary involvement with trademarks, in the licensing field, occurs when rights in a name or a character are sold and incorporated in particular products. (An example would be the use of a character's name in conjunction with a toy modeled on the character. The character or its name could also be licensed for use on decals for mugs, or on heat transfer patches for T-shirts). The character could also be licensed to promote the sale of particular product or service, like a chain of fastfood outlets. Each of the foregoing applications would represent a licensed use of the character as well as the name. The licensing of Mickey Mouse represents one of the longest and most successful character-licensing ventures ever, with Mickey having promoted everything from Chevrolets to disposable diapers.

Unlike copyrights and patents, the rights of trademark are not strictly statutory and need not be registered with any government, state or federal, to be effective, though governmental registrations are available. Trademark protection is available under state laws, as well as under the federal laws known as the Lanham Act. Trademarks are created automatically through adoption and use in connection with the sale of goods or services.

A trademark can exist in perpetuity provided that the trademark continues to be used as a mark to signify the quality of products and services, and so long as the public perceives the mark as an indicator of the source and origin of the goods. The owner of a trademark can prevent others from using the same or a confusingly similar mark or name in connection with the sale of similar goods or services when the use would be likely to cause confusion to the public.

Although federal registration of a trademark is not required to secure protection for the image to be trademarked, in appropriate cases, registration should be made to acquire certain substantive rights and procedural advantages against infringers. Registration constitutes notice of the registrant's claim of ownership; it creates certain presumptions of ownership, validity, and exclusive right to use the mark on the goods recited in the registration; and it establishes criminal penalties for intentionally dealing in products known to be counterfeit.

A federal trademark registration must be made in accordance with prescribed forms available from the Patent and Trademark Office and is filed with that Office. The filing fee for registration is $175 for each class of goods covered by the application. The applicant must select the class of goods for which the mark is being registered. There are 29 merchandising classes of goods, so fees can mount up. These fees do not include the expense of having an attorney prepare the registration application. (Note that it is not required that an attorney prepare the registration, but it is advisable to seek professional advice.)

Before any registration is undertaken, a trademark clearance search should be conducted on the potential trademark to determine if the trademark is available for the intended use. Such a search should be performed by a reputable trademark search firm (usually hired by the lawyer preparing the registration) and it can cost several hundred dollars. However, it makes little sense to invest the time and money necessary to develop a mark and discover later that it is not available for the intended use.

A recent amendment to the trademark law, known as the Trademark Law Revision Act of 1988, effective November 16, 1989, allows trademark registration to be applied for on the basis of the applicant's intention to use a mark. This "intent to use" application permits an individual to reserve a mark and determine if it can be registered before investing heavily in advertising, promotion, and extensive actual use. However, the Trademark Office will not issue a registration until there is a "bona fide use of the mark in the ordinary course of trade." This actual use of the mark can occur up to three years after such an application to register the mark is made, subject to certain 6-month filing requirements.

Trademark registration forms are available from the United States Department of Commerce, Patent and Trademark Office, Washington, D.C. 20231. The booklet "General Information Concerning Trademarks," published by the Office, provides an overview of federal trademarks and contains sample registration forms. A federally registered trademark is valid for an initial 20-year term and can be renewed *ad infinitum* provided the mark is used in accordance with the registration. In order to preserve this registration period, the owner must file an affidavit in the fifth year of use affirming that the mark is still in use. Once a registration is obtained, the owner has to continue to use the mark and must police it to prevent others from using it or a confusingly similar name or risk losing the rights to the mark.

The following notices can be used on federally registered trademarks: ®, "Registered in U.S. Patent and Trademark Office" or "Reg. U.S. Pat. & Tm. Off." Prior to registration, the symbol "TM" may be used with the trademark, signifying rights in the mark.

Over the past several years, expanded judicial interpretations of traditional concepts of trademark have extended new protections to designers for product packaging and labels so that the design itself, referred to as "trade dress," can be protected legally. Trade dress is concerned with the distinctive appearance or look of an item.

The design and appearance of a product may be considered a trademark when these elements serve to identify and distinguish the product from other products. Under current federal trademark law, the physical design of a product may be protected if the physical details and design features of a product are nonfunctional and the public associates the feature with one product source. Some courts even have concluded that where a design is inherently distinctive, the design feature can be protected without this second requirement.

This represents an important development, since copyright ordinarily does not protect product design and because securing a design patent usually is impractical (given the almost immediate need to present ideas and concepts as developed and the length of time necessary to secure a design patent). Use of the principles of trade dress offers a relatively easy way for artists and designers to protect their work when making presentations. Thus, if a product or packaging designer plans to make a presentation, he or she should display an appropriate trademark notice for the materials shown. For example: a designer is asked to prepare a prototype packaging for a jewelry collection. The packaging and all accompanying illustrative materials, whether photographs, sketches, or illustrations, should bear the following notice: "Design Concept and Packaging TM by (name of the designer)." In this way, those viewing the materials are given notice that the designer claims proprietary rights to the creative work and they are not at liberty to use or copy the materials without permission.

Chapter 3

Safeguarding an Idea

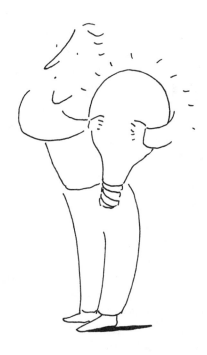

T he dilemma confronting many originators of creative ideas is how to protect the idea and prevent someone from "stealing" it before an agreement is reached for its use, when the idea must be disclosed as a condition for its commercial development. The placement of a copyright or trademark notice (if applicable) on the work and on the accompanying materials will not protect the underlying ideas or concepts. For, as discussed in the preceding chapter, a copyright does not protect an idea, only the expression of an idea, and, ideas alone are not subject to protection under the trademark or patent laws either.

Yet valuable rights exist in ideas—ideas, for example, for a new product design, unique packaging, or new applications of existing images. It is important to remember that the voluntary submission of an unsolicited idea can result in the forfeiture of rights in the idea. This can occur when the disclosure is made in an attempt to interest a promising licensee in a project or to induce a potential licensing agent to represent the artist.

How to Protect an Idea

Over the years, a judicially created "law of ideas" has evolved, which offers a patchwork of protection for artists and designers under certain circumstances. These special circumstances include a legal relationship between the parties, created either by an express, written contract or a contract implied by a course of conduct, or by a fiduciary relationship. In the absence of these special circumstances, an unprotected idea easily can be lost upon disclosure.

The best and easiest way to create a legally protectable circumstance is to have a written contract, known as a "Nondisclosure Agreement," govern the disclosure. A Model Nondisclosure Agreement appears at the end of this chapter.

This agreement is a model form drafted broadly to cover situations where valuable information is to be presented to a party who, in the absence of a promise not to use the information, might appropriate it for pecuniary gain. When signed, the agreement becomes a binding contract giving the originator of the idea the right to commence a lawsuit to stop the unauthorized use or sue for damages for breach of contract if the information disclosed is used without the originator's permission.

The nondisclosure agreement should be used whenever proprietary information is to be revealed. It is appropriate when the information is in the "idea" or "concept" stage as well as when the artist or designer believes the work is protected by a copyright or trademark.

The following example illustrates why a nondisclosure agreement should be used: An illustrator shows a publisher a sketch for a poster depicting a humorous view of the world from a New Yorker's perspective. The sketch bears the illustrator's copyright notice. The publisher rejects the artist's sketch; however, he adopts the idea and commissions another illustrator to draw a poster in the same humorous style and look as the New Yorker version, but from the perspective of an Angelino. This poster sells very well.

The aggrieved illustrator might attempt to bring a lawsuit for copyright infringement against the publisher (and the artist) in federal court; but since it is the style and look and not substantially the same image that was copied, the illustrator might have difficulty proving his case. Other problems would confront the illustrator if an action were brought based on a theory of unfair competition. Unfair competition laws protect against a variety of unfair commercial acts. These include trade name infringement (use of a business name likely to cause confusion with a well-established business), false advertising (copying of trade dress packaging, labeling, and product appearance), and misappropriation (unfairly benefitting from another's efforts). Given the difficulties and high costs of such actions, the illustrator could find himself without a means to redress the wrong.

If, however, a nondisclosure agreement had been signed, the illustrator could go to court on a simple breach of contract theory to enforce its terms. There the illustrator would face the easier task of proving a violation of the nondisclosure agreement. A contract action in state or federal court (if jurisdiction allows) is a less costly alternative to instituting a suit for copyright infringement or unfair competition. Thus, use of a nondisclosure agreement increases an artist's chances of protecting his or her rights.

What to Do if a Company Refuses to Sign an Agreement

Some companies refuse as a matter of policy to sign nondisclosure agreements (especially for unsolicited ideas), allegedly to safeguard themselves against nuisance lawsuits for unjustified claims that they have wrongly appropriated another's idea. However, many of these companies will entertain submissions from individuals on a nonconfidential basis.

These companies require the designer to sign a "submission form" or a "waiver form" (the opposite of the nondisclosure form) whereby the designer waives any rights of any sort in and to the information and materials submitted. It permits the submission of ideas without the creation of a confidential relationship.

Such waivers give a company free reign to develop the information as it sees fit with no obligation to pay the designer. In these circumstances the designer gambles on the company's sense of fair play and trusts that the company will remunerate the designer, although legally it is not obligated to do so. This is risky. Anyone willing to reveal information under these conditions should carefully evaluate the chances of losing the idea to another.

When caution is cast to the wind, and an idea must be disclosed, the following procedures should be followed.

• Document the idea before meeting with a third party by sending a description of the idea to an attorney or trusted friend.

• Mark all submitted (portfolio) materials with the appropriate copyright or trademark or patent notices. See chapter 2 for the correct forms.

• After an appointment is made to present the idea or project, write a self-serving letter to confirm the meeting to discuss the idea (do not disclose the substance of the idea here). Retain a copy of the letter.

• If there is a visitor's log available, upon arrival sign in and note the date and time of arrival.

• Note who is in attendance at the meeting and their positions with the company. Be wary of the presence of marketing or art directors. They may be on the lookout for new ideas to develop in-house.

• If the company wants to pursue the idea or work further, ask for a written proposal for review by your attorney or business advisor.

• Recapitulate the substance of the meeting by writing a letter to the person in charge of the meeting confirming the discussions had. Make reference to the date of the meeting and mention the substance of the information disclosed (i.e., "Thank you for taking the time to meet with me on October 31, 1990, to discuss my ideas for a 'Pet Plant' and its 'Pottie' packaging and your company's marketing and selling of the same ..."). Keep a copy of the letter.

Although there is no iron-clad means to protect against the theft of the disclosed idea or information, these procedures create a paper trail of documentation for the benefit of the originator of the idea. They establish a time sequence that helps demonstrate that the designer originated and introduced the particular idea or item prior to the company's commercial exploitation of it. Should a dispute arise, records can strengthen an artist's position for purposes of settlement. If settlement talks fail and a lawsuit is commenced, the records can be used to fortify the artist's claims in court.

A Note on Employee Agreements

In a related area, it is important to keep in mind that some employers require their salaried employees and the people who work for them as freelancers or consultants to sign confidentiality agreements. A confidentiality agreement may be a separate agreement or a provision contained in an employment agreement. Its operative provisions also can appear on an invoice or job order form.

The essence of a confidentiality provision is that the employee or freelancer acknowledges that, in the course of working for the company, he or she will be exposed to and will acquire valuable confidential information which he or she will not divulge or disclose to or use for the benefit of outsiders without the company's express written permission. Some agreements force the designer or artist to transfer to the employer ownership of all work created during the course of the working relationship as well as all derivative works and related images created and to be created.

These provisions can be invoked by a company to bar an artist or designer from later creating and selling work similar to or based on ideas for work produced during the course of the employment or engagement. Merely altering a work will not absolve the artist from these restrictions if the work contains common elements or themes. If this were to occur, an artist could be forced to change his or her style of work in order to earn a living from the sale of artwork.

MODEL NONDISCLOSURE AGREEMENT

DATE:_____

TO: _____

_____

_____

I am about to disclose to you valuable information, concepts, ideas, designs, and corresponding advertising and packaging which I deem confidential (hereinafter collectively referred to as the "Information").

You understand and acknowledge that the unauthorized disclosure of the Information by you to others would irreparably damage me. In consideration of and in return for my disclosing the Information, you agree to keep it secret and hold the Information in confidence and treat the Information as if it were your own proprietary property, disclosing it to no person or entity.

This disclosure shall be only for purposes of evaluation to determine your interest in the commercial exploitation of the Information. You agree not to manufacture, sell, deal in, or otherwise use or appropriate the disclosed Information in any way whatsoever including, and without limitation, through adaptation, imitation, redesign, or modification.

It is understood that except for this requirement of confidentiality you have no other obligation to me. If, on the basis of your evaluation of the Information, you wish to pursue the exploitation thereof, we each agree to enter into good faith negotiations to arrive at a mutually satisfactory agreement for this purpose. Unless and until such an agreement is entered into, this non-disclosure Agreement shall remain in full force and effect.

This Agreement shall be governed by the laws of the State of _____ and shall be binding upon and shall inure to our benefit and to the benefit of our respective legal representatives, successors, and assigns. Nothing herein shall be deemed to give you any rights or interest whatsoever in and to the Information.

_____
Artist/Designer

ACCEPTED AND AGREED TO:

_____
Signature of Individual

_____
Corporation

By:_____
      (name and position)

Chapter 4

The Licensing Agreement Analyzed

The commentary which follows analyzes a suggested Model Long Form Licensing Agreement completed to reflect a simulated licensing arrangement. The Model Long Form Agreement and a suggested shorter version are printed in full in chapter 5. It is recommended that the reader refer to the Model Long Form Agreement while reading the analysis so that continuity of the agreement is maintained.

The analysis of the model agreement is designed to help untangle the legal and business aspects covered in such a document and illumine the negotiating process. Not every provision should be used in every license arrangement. The agreement and commentary can serve as a guide to help develop an agreement customized for individual needs. This agreement is not limited to designs for T-shirts. It can be adapted for any licensed property. A design firm, as well as individuals, can use this agreement, but its principals must make sure that the firm owns the rights in the designs and artwork before the work is licensed.

In this simulation, the licensor is a successful graphic designer who has built up considerable name recognition for herself and her designs. She presents the licensee/T-shirt manufacturing company with an overall concept: "Cities-by-the-Sea," consisting of five designs, each separately named, which support the theme. The company is among a handful of well-regarded producers of high quality T-shirts.

The agreement is an exclusive license covering designs and trademarks for an initial term of two years with an option to extend the term for another two-year period upon the satisfaction of certain conditions. The subject designs, term, territory, identification of licensed products, as well as reimbursements for certain costs of production, are set forth in Schedule A. This is done for ease of negotiating, though admittedly the placement of specific items is subjective, and could be set forth in the main body of the text. There is no such item as a "Standard Licensing Agreement" any more than there is a "Standard Lease." The artist is free to develop what is best suited for him or her.

These operational criteria are not atypical of those encountered in practice. The provisions selected were chosen because of the particular facts of this licensing deal. The final terms and conditions of an actual agreement would, of course, be subject to extensive negotiation and one should not expect that every suggested provision could be incorporated in that agreement.

Licensing Agreement Between Sally Stevens and Geoart Inc., dated May 1, 1990

1. Grant of License

AGREEMENT MADE this 1st day of May 1990 between SALLY STEVENS, having an address at One Tribeca South, New York, New York (the "Licensor") and GEOART INC., a New York corporation located at Two Soho South, New York, New York (the "Licensee") whereby Licensor grants to Licensee a license to use the designs listed on the attached Schedules A and B (the "Designs") in accordance with the terms and conditions of this Agreement and only for the production, sale, advertising and promotion of certain articles (the "Licensed Products"), described in Schedule A for the Term and in the Territory set forth in said Schedule. Licensee shall have the right to affix the Trademarks "SALLY STEVENS™" and "CITIES-BY-THE-SEA™" on or to the Licensed Products and on packaging, advertising, and promotional materials sold, used, or distributed in connection with the Licensed Products.

The kernel of the license agreement is the grant of rights. It should describe as specifically as possible the licensed property and the scope of the license not only by enumerating which rights are being transferred but by setting forth the additional qualifiers: whether the license is exclusive or nonexclusive; the length of its term; and the permitted articles on which the licensed property can be reproduced.

The grant here, as qualified by Schedule A, provides for five designs to be used on a range of merchandise: T-shirts, tote bags, coffee mugs, and postcards, for a period of two years. Each design is licensed for a very specific territory: New York, Boston, San Francisco, New Orleans, and Los Angeles respectively. The licensee has the additional right to use the trademarks "Sally Stevens™" and "Cities-by-the-Sea™" on the licensed products and on related promotional items. The licensee should pay for the right to use these trademarks (in the form of an increased royalty), especially if the trademark is well recognized and use of it in association with the licensed products will enhance product sales.

The definition of the rights transferred is very important. Vague descriptions of rights or licensed products are open invitations for confusion. Imprecision can result in the granting of greater rights than intended with the resultant loss of royalties due to the unintentional cede of those rights. Overly broad categories of licensed products should be avoided. Notice that the unambiguous word "T-shirts" is used instead of "shirts." The generic word "shirts" could be construed to include "sweatshirts."

Here is the danger. The designer may have wanted to license the design for use on sweatshirts to another manufacturer and at a royalty rate higher than that for T-shirts, for example 10.5 percent versus 8.5 percent. Geoart Inc. could prevent the second license by arguing that its exclusive license covers sweatshirts. The designer could lose out on royalty income for reasons not apparent initially. The 2 percent difference could cost more than the mere difference on its face, because typically a sweatshirt sells at twice the price of a T-shirt. The loss would be greater. Two percent on a wholesale price of $4.50 yields 9 cents per shirt while 2 percent on $9.00 yields 18 cents per shirt, or, stated another way, 8.5 percent on $4.50 is $ .38 and 10.5 percent on $9.00 is $ .95, and the loss per shirt would be $ .57.

Another risk for the designer might be that she would have to share her royalties from the sweatshirt license with Geoart Inc. or have to negotiate a buy-back of her rights from Geoart Inc. She could wait until her license with Geoart Inc. expires or terminates before entering into the sweatshirt license, but she risks losing the opportunity of a licensing deal because this second licensee may not want to wait two or more years for its license. The Cities-by-the-Sea line could be old hat by then and no longer have sufficient value to justify a license. On the other hand, if the designs are strong and public recognition great, the sweatshirt company might be willing to wait.

Deciding whether to grant an exclusive or nonexclusive license should be considered from the onset. An exclusive license is one where the licensee is the only party who possesses the right to use the licensed property on the licensed articles (if the owner wants to use the design this right must be specifically reserved). A nonexclusive license will permit the owner to grant the same or overlapping licenses, typically with some minor variations, to others. See the discussion regarding paragraph 7.

As a general rule, a licensee should be willing to pay more for an exclusive arrangement to sell a licensed product (knowing that it will not have to worry about competition from another company) than for a nonexclusive license which would permit others to sell the same designs on the same articles. This greater payment could be reflected in a higher royalty rate, or guaranteed royalties, or some additional benefit, like the promise to commit a substantial advertising budget for the promotion and sale of the licensed product. Also, the artist's agreement to be the exclusive artist for a company enhances that company's reputation (the artist has selected it above all others) and, accordingly, the exclusive licensee should pay for this benefit.

The exclusivity addressed here may be an exclusivity aimed at preventing the design from being used on any product or just on competitive products. Bear in mind that a manufacturer who seeks an exclusive license may also want that license to be as broad as possible. This may be the case even though the licensee does not possess the manufacturing capability to produce all the products subsumed in the broad category group. What it hopes to do (through investment in and promotion of the designs) is to create market demand for the same designs on other products. Once this synergistic effect begins, the licensee could sublicense (if sublicensing is permitted—see later discussion at paragraph 15B) to produce the additional products for sale.

In this example, Geoart Inc. is a nationally known manufacturer and distributor of souvenir T-shirts. It has no facilities to produce mugs, totes, or postcards, but because of its extensive exposure at stores and airports throughout the country, it believes retailers would sell these complementary products. Finding a manufacturer would not be difficult. Thus to insure that it will not encounter competition from others, Geoart Inc. would seek exclusive rights covering a wider product range. To implement this plan, it would seek the right to sublicense the exclusive rights it secured from the designer. Having the right to sublicense would enable it to authorize others (for example, the tote or postcard producer) to produce the licensed designs on these additional products. (See continuing discussion on sublicensing at paragraph 15B.)

Sublicensing raises another key consideration for a licensor. Knowing who the potential licensee is, learning about its manufacturing and distribution capabilities, and checking its financial condition are essential. Any weakness in these areas suggests that the license should be a nonexclusive one, leaving the designer free to enter into other agreements.

The dates the license begins and ends, as well as any conditions for termination and options to extend the term, must be clearly specified. This information is set forth in paragraph 3 of Schedule A, and paragraph 11 of this agreement, and explanatory background is given in these provisions.

2. Licensor's Representation and Credits

A. Licensor warrants that Licensor has the right to grant to the Licensee all of the rights conveyed in this Agreement. The Licensee shall have no right, license, or permission except as herein expressly granted. All rights not specifically transferred by this Agreement are reserved to the Licensor.

This provision combines a warranty and ownership provision with a licensor's reservation of rights provision. With respect to the warranty, the licensee seeks the assurance that the rights being conveyed by the licensor are in fact owned by the artist and have not been conveyed to any one else. This is applicable to both exclusive and nonexclusive licenses.

The wording of this first sentence favors the artist since it requires the artist to represent that only she owns what she is licensing. Another more extensive (and not unexpected) provision might read as follows:

Licensor warrants that the Designs are original creations of the Licensor, that the Licensor knows of no adverse claims to or in such Designs, that neither such Designs nor any parts thereof are in the public domain, and that the Designs do not violate the right of publicity or other personal rights of others.

Here the artist is asked to make several representations which go beyond simple copyright ownership. It is reasonable for a licensee to demand these assurances.

Designers must pay close attention to the wording of the representation and find out whether or not it can be enforced after the agreement terminates or expires. If the warranty provision is breached, the artist can be held liable for the consequences of the breach. License agreements often contain indemnification provisions which seek to hold the artist liable for all expenses (such as court costs, attorney's fees, and damages) incurred by the licensee because the artist violated this representation. For what indemnification is, see the discussion for paragraph 11. In addition, some licensees demand the right to withhold payment of accrued royalties to the artist in the event that there is a "claim" that the artist violated the warranty.

The delineation of the rights conveyed and those reserved is set forth in the remaining portion of this paragraph. The reservation of rights also should be clearly set forth.

B. The Licensee prominently shall display and identify the Licensor as the designer on each Licensed Product and on all packaging, advertising, displays, and in all publicity therefor and shall have reproduced thereon (or on an approved tag or label) the following notices:
" © SALLY STEVENS 1990. All rights reserved." and "SALLY STEVENS™." The Licensed Products shall be marketed under the name SALLY STEVENS™ for GEOART INC. The name SALLY STEVENS™ shall not be cojoined with any third party's name without the Licensor's express written permission

This "legal notice" provision, in addition to setting forth the various notices in the required forms, also further clarifies the grant of rights. In this case, the designer sets the terms and conditions for the use of her trademarks. In addition to satisfying the various statutory requirements under the copyright and trademark laws, the requirement of notice furthers the designer's reputation by ensuring that her name is associated with the designs and products.

If the licensed product qualifies for design patent protection, the licensor can require the additional patent notices: "patent pending" or "patent applied for." There is no legal requirement to use such a notice; however, once the patent issues the proper patent notice: "U. S. Patent No. _____" must be used or important rights can be forfeited.

The prohibition against cojoining of names with a third party is to avoid the implication of a permitted sublicense or an unpermitted expansion of trademark rights. An example of a cojoining of names is: "SALLY STEVENS™ for GEOART INC. for BREEZE TEES."

> **C.** The Licensee shall have the right to use the Licensor's name, portrait, or picture in a dignified manner, consistent with the Licensor's reputation, in advertising or other promotional materials associated with the sale of the Licensed Products.

The licensee may want to use the licensor's photograph in advertising materials to promote the sale of the licensed products. So as not to violate numerous states' right to privacy and publicity laws, this permission is essential. In general, these laws protect individuals from having their names and portraits used for trade or advertising purposes without their permission.

The artist or designer should accommodate this request, provided the use is in a dignified manner consistent with the designer's reputation. In some circumstances, when the artist possesses great notoriety, as Andy Warhol did during his lifetime, the right to use the artist's picture or portrait as an endorsement may justify the payment of additional compensation.

3. Royalties and Statements of Account

A. Licensee agrees to pay Licensor a nonrefundable royalty of seven (7%) percent of the net sales of all of the Licensed Products incorporating and embodying the Designs. "Net sales" is defined as sales direct to customers less prepaid freight and credits for lawful and customary volume rebates, actual returns, and allowances. The aggregate of said deductions and credits shall not exceed three (3%) percent of accrued royalties in any year. No costs incurred in the manufacture, sale, distribution, or exploitation of the Licensed Products shall be deducted from any royalties due to Licensor. Royalties shall be deemed to accrue when the Licensed Products are sold, shipped, or invoiced, whichever first occurs.

B. Royalty payments for all sales shall be due on the 15th day after the end of each calendar quarter. At that time and regardless if any Licensed Products were sold during the preceding time period, Licensee shall furnish Licensor with an itemized statement categorized by Design, showing the kinds and quantities of all Licensed Products sold and the prices received therefor, and all deductions for freight, volume rebates, returns, and allowances. The first royalty statement shall commence on October 1, 1990.

C. If Licensor has not received the royalty payment as required by the foregoing Paragraph 3B within 21 days following the end of each calendar quarter, a monthly service charge of one-and-a-half (1.5%) percent shall accrue thereon and become due and owing from the date on which such royalty payment became due and owing.

The royalty arrangement lies at the heart of every licensing deal. From each party's perspective it is one of the most important provisions, as it establishes the financial arrangement between them.

The rate of royalties and any advances or minimum guaranteed royalties must be considered and carefully coordinated with the overall marketing plan for the designs. Since the designer's income is based on either a percentage of sales or a fixed sum per item sold, before agreeing to a royalty rate, the designer should request marketing data such as the projected selling price of the licensed items, the expected annual gross sales, and selling plans, in order to set a corresponding rate and maximize income. The licensor is entitled to this information. A high royalty rate can become a ghost rate if the goods do not sell well because they are overpriced for the intended market or the licensee has poor distribution.

Paragraphs 3 and 4 set forth the minimum conditions which a license agreement should contain, namely, provisions which enumerate: the royalty rate used to calculate actual payments to the licensor; the basis for the calculation of the royalties; an itemization of permissible deductions; specification of information to be contained in royalty statements; and the date when payment and statements are due.

The royalty rate can be structured as a percentage of the price of products sold or as a fixed sum per item sold. Because a fixed rate formula will not match the rate of inflation over the term of the license, a percentage rate would be more favorable to the licensor, as the royalty automatically adjusts when the licensee raises prices.

One of the biggest misconceptions in licensing is the commonly held belief that there are "standard" royalty rates. This is plainly not the case. Royalty rates are the result of negotiation. They vary from product to product, licensor to licensor, licensee to licensee, territory to territory, and marketing plan to marketing plan. The royalty rate is also subject to such variables as the amount of minimum royalties guaranteed, the amount of the advance, and the licensee's payment of design fees and other production costs.

The danger of discussing representative royalty rates, such as those on the chart of comparative average royalties that appears in the Appendices, is that the examples will be taken as gospel when they function only as rough guidelines. To say that a licensor obtained 15 percent for a license of a puppet character, or Warner Brothers received between 5 and 10 percent for licenses of the "Batman" character, or that most greeting card companies pay between 2 to 3 percent of wholesale sales really is meaningless. Each license must be evaluated against the constellation of variables discussed above and throughout this analysis.

The license should clearly state the basis on which the royalty is calculated. Typically, royalties are calculated on "net sales," as in paragraph 3A. Pay particular attention to the definition of the terms or basis of calculation. Avoid fuzzy open-ended provisions like "based on sales"—what kinds of sales: gross, wholesale, retail, or discount? What deductions are permitted? Can the licensee retain royalties as a reserve against damaged or returned items? Some licensees routinely deduct an arbitrary 10 percent of accrued royalties from royalty payments to cover expected returns. This should be avoided. No deductions should be allowed for cash sales, discounts, or seller's commissions.

The licensor should always make sure that the royalties are nonrefundable to avoid having to pay money back if returns exceed sales in the case of a defect in the product or if the licensing program fails.

Lastly, when the royalty becomes due should be defined. A royalty can become due when the product is invoiced for sale, when it is shipped, or when payment is received by the licensee. Paragraph 3A signals payment on the earliest occurrence of any one of these events.

4. Advances and Minimum Royalties

A. In each year of this Agreement, Licensee agrees to pay Licensor a Guaranteed Minimum Royalty of $10,000, of which $5,000 shall be deemed a Nonrefundable Advance against royalties. The difference, if any, between the Guaranteed Minimum Royalty and the Advance shall be divided equally and paid quarterly over the term of this Agreement commencing with the quarter beginning October I, 1990.

B. The Nonrefundable Advance shall be paid on the signing of this Agreement. No part of the Guaranteed Minimum Royalty or the Nonrefundable Advance shall be repayable to Licensee.

C. Licensor has the right to terminate this Agreement upon the giving of thirty (30) days' notice to Licensee if the Licensee fails to pay any portion of the Guaranteed Minimum Royalty when due.

When negotiating the royalty rate, it is advisable to bargain for an advance on the payment of royalties and the payment of a guaranteed minimum royalty. This is true particularly when an exclusive license is granted. The payment compensates the designer for declining other licenses involving the licensed work. The licensee should be willing to make this payment in exchange for the security of not having to deal with competitive licenses. The minimum guaranteed royalty could be a fixed amount paid over the term as in the above example, or it could increase each year of the license to reflect an anticipated increase in accrued royalties.

Advances and guaranteed minimum royalty payments vary widely depending on work licensed and the reputations of the licensee and licensor. For this reason, there are no set figures. The amount of the advance and any guarantees is subject to negotiation. As a rule of thumb, the starting point for determining the minimum guaranty should be the average amount of projected royalties. If a licensee is unwilling to back up its forecast of royalties with a corresponding guaranty, this reluctance should cause the licensor to scrutinize the licensee more closely.

In most licensing arrangements, when an advance is paid it is assumed that the advance collectively covers all the designs subject to the agreement. This may not be the designer's intent. If multiple designs are subject to the agreement, the designer may want to specify that an advance is to be paid for each design. Paragraph 4A can be modified to accomplish this as follows:

> On the signing of this Agreement, Licensee agrees to pay to Licensor a nonrefundable Advance against royalties in the amount of $_____ for each Design licensed.

This alternate language benefits the designer in another way. It provides for a minimum royalty payment on each of the licensed designs rather than on all of the designs cumulatively. What's the difference? There could be a situation involving five designs in which design #1 is very hot and is outselling the others by a large margin; royalties on designs #2, #3, and #4 are even with the guaranteed minimum for each; and design #5 has not sold well at all. This provision would ensure the payment of a minimum royalty on design #5, without deduction from the royalties on design #1 that are in excess of design #1's minimum; that is, no portion of the royalties which accrued on the other designs will be applied to the payment of design #5's minimum. This would assure payment of the minimum royalty and leave accrued royalties in excess of each individual design's guarantee untouched.

Sometimes a licensee will not pay an advance. If this occurs, suggest the payment of a design fee instead. A design fee is simply a payment for the design. It is a one-time payment and should not be treated as a royalty payment. The following language can be incorporated into the agreement if this is appropriate:

> On signing of this Agreement, Licensee shall pay Licensor a nonrefundable design fee in the amount of $_____ per Design. This fee shall not be applied against royalties.

However structured, advances, guaranteed royalties, and design fees should be made nonrefundable, and the nonpayment of any of these fees should be set forth as a ground to terminate the license immediately.

5. Books and Records

Licensee agrees to keep complete and accurate books and records relating to the sale and other distribution of each of the Licensed Products. Licensor or its representative shall have the right to inspect Licensee's books and records relating to the sales of the Licensed Products upon thirty (30) days prior written notice. Any discrepancies over 5% between the royalties received and the royalties due will be subject to the royalty payment set forth herein and paid immediately. If the audit discloses such an underpayment of 10% or more, Licensee shall reimburse the Licensor for all the costs of said audit.

The obligation to keep separate books and records relating to the sale of the licensed products should not surprise any businessman. Neither should a request for the right to audit these materials. Should the licensee either fail to pay royalties or remit amounts less than expected, the artist would want the right to examine the books and records prior to commencing a lawsuit to seek an accounting. When invoked, this right to audit may precipitate the payment of past due royalties. Without this right, the only way a licensor could obtain this information would be by a court-ordered accounting, a lengthy and expensive procedure. Any underpayments disclosed by the audit should be paid immediately; and the costs of the audit should be paid for by the licensee if the underpayment exceeds a certain dollar amount or 10 percent of the royalties due.

6. Quality of Licensed Products, Approval, and Advertising

A. Licensee agrees that the Licensed Products shall be of the highest standard and quality and of such style and appearance as to be best suited to their exploitation to the best advantage and to the protection and enhancement of the Licensed Products and the good will pertaining thereto. The Licensed Products shall be manufactured, sold, and distributed in accordance with all applicable national, state, and local laws.

B. In order to insure that the development, manufacture, appearance, quality, and distribution of each Licensed Product is consonant with the Licensor's good will associated with its reputation, copyrights, and trademarks, Licensor shall have the right to approve in advance the quality of the Licensed Products (including, without limitation, concepts and preliminary prototypes, mechanicals or camera-ready art prior to production of first sample; production sample and revised production sample, if any) and all packaging, literature, advertising, publicity, promotion, and displays for the Licensed Products.

C. Licensee shall be responsible for delivering all items requiring prior approval pursuant to Paragraph 6B without cost to the Licensor. Licensor agrees not to withhold approval unreasonably.

D. Licensee shall not release or distribute any Licensed Product without securing each of the prior approvals provided for in Paragraph 6B. Licensee shall not depart from any approval secured in accordance with Paragraph 6B without Licensor's prior written consent.

A paramount concern of the designer or artist should be the quality of the finished product. Not to be overlooked is the quality of the packaging and promotional and advertising materials, which can be as important as the licensed product.

Whether it is the poor quality of the inking on a screenprint for a T-shirt, or the inattentiveness to detail on a jewelry piece, badly executed work impacts negatively on both the artistic and business reputations of the licensor. The proper exercise of quality control necessitates the artist's involvement and exchange of approvals during the entire production process, from sketch to finished product and packaging.

The quality control provisions here are more elaborate than most licensing agreements because practice has shown that the approval requirement often gets shunted aside. Typically what can happen is that the manufacturer agrees to have the designer approve the sample of the work, but the request for approval is sent out late. By the time the designer receives the samples and disapproves a sample—perhaps because of minor color variations which, though not satisfactory to the artist, are commercially acceptable—the licensee has proceeded with the run and claims it is too late to do anything to stop it.

After some protest, the designer unhappily accepts the product. Why? Because "It's not worth the delay in getting the product to market," or "It's not worth the legal expense to hire an attorney to threaten to hold the licensee in breach if it does not correct the situation," or any other variation. The control provisions are only effective insofar as the licensor chooses to enforce them.

Here, the minimum standard "highest quality" is supported by a sequence of detailed approvals, requiring, among other items, that the licensee not deviate from approved versions except with the licensor's consent. This agreement contains a specially developed "Approval Schedule" (see Schedule C). It is intended to keep the licensor actively involved during the entire manufacturing process. If used as prescribed, it offers a methodical procedure to monitor the licensed work in progress.

Maintaining artistic control means more than the artist's retaining the right to approve the final product. It means that the licensor does not forfeit artistic freedom, and also that the licensor protects the right to earn a living from the sale of designs and from the exploitation of the designer's reputation and name. Some designers sign agreements containing restrictive clauses that limit their rights to use their names in connection with the sale of any products in other agreements. The restriction can be for the term of the agreement and can be written to survive expiration and even termination for cause by the designer. These restrictions are onerous and should be avoided.

One nationally known designer found himself in this unpleasant situation after his agreement with a major retail store was terminated. The agreement signed prevented him from using his name in association with any product for a number of years. He could not enter into other licensing agreements using his name during the blackout period. However, during that time, the store, which secured the right to use his name on products it sold, placed his name on a myriad of products (high-end as well as low-end) and the designer had no legal recourse to stop them.

> **E.** In each year of this Agreement, Licensee shall expend at least .25% percent of anticipated gross sales of the Licensed Products to promote and advertise sales of the Licensed Products.

An important component of a successful licensing program is the licensee's commitment to promote the product, and, sometimes, the designer's name as well. If a licensee wants an exclusive relationship, the designer may well exact a guarantee of expenditures for promotional activities.

The type of campaign and amount of funds, and whether such a provision is even appropriate, will vary considerably depending on the designer, the design, and the products licensed. An exclusive license for a newly created line of watches for sale in upscale shops would seemingly justify a larger expenditure than would a nonexclusive license for designs of mass market T-shirts. Similarly, expenses for personal appearances by the designer supported by sophisticated print ads placed in select magazines may be more appropriate for the watch license than for the T-shirt license. There are no hard and fast rules. Any special requirement should be set forth in the agreement as is required in point 7 in Schedule A.

If the licensee provides projections of anticipated gross sales, incorporate them into the agreement. The figure of .25 percent of "anticipated gross sales" inserted here is based on expected gross sales of $250,000 over two years. This is very generous for T-shirts because T-shirts basically advertise and sell themselves. The approximate expenditure of $625 per city each year would cover some minimal advertising costs. Note that the costs for an ad for the T-shirts placed in a national magazine could exhaust this sum easily. Remember, the advertising figure is always subject to negotiation. It should bear a reasonable relationship to the type of product licensed and estimated advertising costs. The details of when and how the advertising or promotion is to be undertaken should be specified.

7. Nonexclusive Rights

> Nothing in this Agreement shall be construed to prevent Licensor from granting other licenses for the use of the Designs or from utilizing the Designs in any manner whatsoever, except that the Licensor shall not grant other Licenses for the use of the Designs in connection with the sale of the Licensed Products in the Territory to which this License extends during the term of this Agreement.

This provision supports the licensor's reservation of rights in the nature of a nonexclusive license (see commentary for paragraphs 1 and 2) but curtails the designer's freedom to grant certain licenses in the territory covered by the agreement. In practice, this means the designer is free to grant someone else the right to use the five designs on T-shirts for sale outside Boston, New York, New Orleans, San Francisco, and Los Angeles. In this case, this may be an empty right because each design is city specific. However, the designer could grant licenses to other licensees in the respective territories to products other than the covered products, such as travel posters.

8. Nonacquisition of Rights

The Licensee's use of the Designs and Trademarks shall inure to the benefit of the Licensor. If Licensee acquires any trade rights, trademarks, equities, titles, or other rights in and to the Designs or in the Trademark, by operation of law, usage, or otherwise during the term of this Agreement or any extension thereof, Licensee shall forthwith upon the expiration of this Agreement or any extension thereof or sooner termination, assign and transfer the same to Licensor without any consideration other than the consideration of this Agreement.

There is always the risk under a licensing arrangement that the licensee may acquire rights in the designs and in the trademarks through use of the same under the license. This happens unintentionally—for example, under the trademark laws a user acquires rights in a trademark through mere use. To avoid the loss of any rights through the exercise of the license, this provision has the licensee recognize that any rights in and to the designs and trademarks inure, that is belong to, the licensor. It further requires the licensee to assign any rights acquired by any means back to the owner (the licensor), upon request, and without the owner having to buy them back.

9. Licensee's Representations

The Licensee warrants and represents that during the term of this License and for any time thereafter, it, or any of its affiliated, associated, or subsidiary companies will not copy or imitate or authorize the imitation or copying of the Designs, Tradenames, and Trademarks, or any distinctive feature of the foregoing or other designs submitted to the Licensee by Licensor. Without prejudice to any other remedies the Licensor may have, royalties as provided herein shall accrue and be paid by Licensee on all items embodying and incorporating imitated or copied Designs.

A provision like this one is intended to protect the artist against adverse acts by the licensee with respect to unauthorized copying or appropriation of the designs by the licensee and related third parties. It functions as a warning not to exceed the grant of the license directly or indirectly through subterfuge by the licensee, its affiliates, or related companies. This paragraph provides a basis for the termination of the license (see paragraph 12A), a cause of action for a lawsuit against any of the parties violating the provision, and allows the designer to elect to receive royalties on the imitations or copies sold at the same rates as those provided under the agreement, without prejudice to any other rights and remedies the licensor may have.

The last sentence of this provision is intended to cover a situation in which the manufacturer makes a change in the design. For example, without notifying the designer, Geoart Inc. changes the colors (because of printing difficulties) from the approved color scheme and sells shirts with this change. Technically this variation is a new design which Geoart Inc. is not licensed to sell. However, because the changed shirt meets the designer's artistic standard, rather than terminate the entire license on the grounds that Geoart Inc. exceeded the terms of the license, this provision allows the licensor to permit the sale and to collect royalties. At the same time the designer reserves the right to seek damages in court if appropriate.

10. Registrations and Infringements

A. The Licensor has the right but not the obligation to obtain at its own cost appropriate copyright, trademark, and patent protection for the Designs and the Trademarks. At Licensor's request and at Licensee's sole cost and expense, Licensee shall make all necessary and appropriate registrations to protect the copyrights, trademarks, and patents in and to the Licensed Products and the advertising, promotional, and packaging material in the Territory in which the Licensed Products are sold. Copies of all applications shall be submitted for approval to Licensor prior to filing. The Licensee and Licensor agree to cooperate with each other to assist in the filing of said registrations.

B. Licensee shall not at any time apply for or abet any third party to apply for copyright, trademark, or patent protection which would affect Licensor's ownership of any rights in the Designs or the Trademarks.

The obligation to obtain necessary registrations to protect the designs and trademarks can be either the licensor's or the licensee's, depending on the circumstances. It is usually in the designer's best interests to insure that the designs and trademarks are protected and to make the filings.

Often a potential licensee will not negotiate if these protections have not been secured by the time the license is signed. It is comforting, too, for the designer to know that the filed registrations contain no conflicting or adverse recitals which might be included if the licensee does the filing. To guard against this happening, the agreement under analysis requires prior submissions to the licensor before filings.

The costs of trademark and most certainly design patent registrations, unlike those of copyright registration, are considerable. They may amount to over several thousand dollars (see chapter 2). Aside from not being able to afford these costs, the licensor may find that undertaking such expenses at the preliminary stage—without a license in hand—does not make sense. Even if the license were secured, anticipated royalties might not be sufficient to justify the expenditure.

The provision here effects a compromise. It lets the designer choose whether or not to make the registrations. If the designer chooses not to act, the designer can request and require the licensee to file the registrations at its expense.

Some negotiation can be expected on this point. The licensee will most likely seek some sharing of these expenses. If the licensee insists on this, perhaps it would be willing to advance the designer's share as a credit against royalties.

The last sentence of this paragraph is intended to prevent the licensee (especially an exclusive licensee) from attempting to register in its own name and claim ownership rights in the licensed property by virtue of its exclusive license. This would challenge the designer's ownership of the property and must be avoided.

C. Licensee shall notify Licensor in writing immediately upon discovery of any infringements or imitations by others of the Designs, Tradenames, or Trademarks. Licensor in its sole discretion may bring any suit, action, or proceeding Licensor deems appropriate to protect Licensor's rights in the Designs, Tradenames, and Trademarks, including, without limitation, for copyright and trademark infringement and for unfair competition. If, for any reason, Licensor does not institute any such suit or take any such action or proceeding, upon written notice to the Licensee, Licensee may institute such appropriate suit, action, or proceeding in Licensee's and Licensor's names. In any event, Licensee and Licensor shall cooperate fully with each other in the prosecution of such suit, action, or proceeding. Licensor reserves the right, at Licensor's cost and expense, to join in any pending suit, action, or proceeding. The instituting party shall pay all costs and expenses, including legal fees, incurred by the instituting party. All recoveries and awards, including settlements received, after payments of costs and legal fees, shall be divided seventy-five (75%) percent to the instituting party and twenty-five (25%) percent to the other party.

It happens. Through no fault of the licensee, the designs appear on travel posters without permission. Whose obligation is it to take action, to place the infringer on notice that it is violating the copyright of the designer? Can the licensee initiate action without the knowledge or consent of the licensor? Who should undertake the costs of engaging an attorney or underwriting the costs of a lawsuit? How should any recovery be allocated?

The answers to these and related questions ought to be provided by the license agreement, should an infringement or other violation of the licensed work occur. In the absence of an agreement, the licensee usually does not have "standing" as required by law to commence an action for such infringements.

This paragraph gives the licensor the right but not the obligation to pursue such an action. Many times, intervention by the copyright owner is not warranted—the infringement is too minor, or, if significant, the slim chance of recovering monetary damages does not justify the legal expense.

These considerations, however, might not apply to the licensee. Because the licensee has expended sizable sums in connection with the license (production costs and creation of a market), it does not want its efforts and good will appropriated by another. Many companies realize that vigorous policing of their purchased rights is essential to prevent loss of rights through inaction. Others regularly bring actions against infringers to maintain their established reputations of not tolerating knock-offs of their products. So, for these companies, the right to proceed against an infringer is a must. This paragraph allows such a company to do so with expenses and recoveries allocated equitably.

11. Indemnification and Insurance

A. The Licensee hereby agrees to indemnify and hold the Licensor harmless against all liability, cost, loss, expense (including reasonable attorneys' fees), or damage paid, incurred, or occasioned by any claim, demand, suit, settlement, or recovery against the Licensor, without limitation, arising out of the breach or claim of breach of this Agreement; the unauthorized use of the Designs by it or any third party; the manufacture, distribution, and sale of the Licensed Products; and for any alleged defects in the Licensed Products. Licensee hereby consents to submit to the personal jurisdiction of any court, tribunal, or forum in which an action or proceeding is brought involving a claim to which this foregoing indemnification shall apply.

Indemnification provisions similar to this one routinely are being included in agreements and relied on with ever increasing frequency. Accordingly, artists and designers ought to be aware of the existence of these provisions and understand the consequences.

An indemnification provision functions like an insurance policy to protect against claims and expenses made against a party by others. The indemnification here is for the benefit of the designer, to protect the licensor from any expense and liability which may arise from Geoart Inc.'s breach of the agreement or claims of third parties asserted against the licensor.

It would not be unexpected for a licensee to request a provision from the designer requiring indemnification for breaches of the designer's warranties or representations. It would be appropriate for the licensee to receive an assurance that:

> The designs licensed are original; the Licensor is the copyright owner of the designs; and the designs do not violate the rights of any person.

This assurance would be backed up by the designer's indemnification that if the licensor breached this warranty, the licensor would be liable to the licensee for expenses incurred as a result of the breached provision. If the licensee insists on the artist's indenmifying it, try to limit financial exposure to royalties received.

> **B.** Licensee shall obtain at its sole cost and expense product liability insurance in an amount providing sufficient and adequate coverage, but not less than $1,000,000, combined single limit coverage protecting the Licensor against any claims or lawsuits arising from alleged defects in the Licensed Product.

Even though the contract's indemnification provision should protect a designer against incurring costs for product liability actions brought by injured third parties, it is better practice to require the licensee to carry product liability insurance with adequate coverage and with low deductibles. Obviously, the riskier the product licensed the greater is the need for higher insurance coverage. It is less likely that a person would injure himself with a T-shirt than with a designer dart gun, but one never knows so insurance is appropriate.

12. Grounds for and Consequences of Termination

> **A.** Licensor shall have the right to terminate this Agreement by written notice, whereupon all the rights granted to the Licensee shall revert forthwith to the Licensor and all royalties or other payments shall become due and payable immediately if:

i. Licensee fails to comply with or fulfill any of the terms or conditions of this Agreement;

ii. the Licensed Products have not been offered or made available for sale by Licensee three (3) months from the date hereof;

iii. Licensee ceases to manufacture and sell the Licensed Products in commercially reasonable quantities; or

iv. the Licensee is adjudicated a bankrupt, makes an assignment for the benefit of creditors, or liquidates its business.

B. Licensee, as quickly as possible, but in no event later than thirty (30) days after such termination, shall submit to Licensort the statements required in Paragraph 3 for all sales and distributions through the date of termination. Licensor shall have the right to conduct an actual inventory on the date of termination or thereafter to verify the accuracy of said statements.

C. In the event of termination, all payments theretofore made to the Licensor shall belong to the Licensor without prejudice to any other remedies the Licensor may have.

It is exceedingly important for the licensor to be able to terminate the entire license quickly and easily if the arrangement sours because the licensee violates a material provision of the contract. This might occur when the licensee uses the designs in a manner not approved by the licensor, exceeds the selling territory, creates a knock-off line of similar designs, sublicenses without permission, or fails to meet a critical marketing date. It is recommended that the licensor specify the grounds for termination which are important to the particular deal (such as the initial marketing date here, three months after May 1, 1990, a date which is coordinated with the production date set forth in Schedule A, point 5).

In the event of a breach serious enough to justify an immediate termination of the agreement, it is important for the designer to have the power to accelerate the payment of accrued royalties and payments, such as unpaid advances or minimum guarantees, and have them paid on termination.

Under conditions when there is a less serious breach of the agreement—for example, inadequate promotion of the exclusively licensed article in a particular territory—the license agreement can give the licensee an opportunity to correct or "cure" the breach if the licensee corrects the violation within a thirty-day period. The license would terminate if the violation were not corrected. Sometimes, less drastic action could be agreed upon by the parties. Thus, for example, rather than terminate the contract entirely, the parties could agree to convert the exclusive license into a nonexclusive one in the particular territory.

13. Sell-Off Right

Provided Licensee is not in default of any term or condition of this Agreement, Licensee shall have the right for a period of six (6) months from the expiration of this Agreement or any extension thereof to sell inventory on hand subject to the terms and conditions of this Agreement, including the payment of royalties and guaranteed minimum royalties on sales which continue during this additional period.

Often, when a license expires by its own terms, there remains unsold inventory or products in the process of being manufactured. Although there may be an implied right of the licensee to dispose of the inventory in accordance with the terms of the license agreement, it is always better practice to specify such a right if one is intended. This disposal right should be conditioned on current payment of royalties, and, when possible, upon the payment of minimum royalties. A sell-off period of between one and six months is reasonable, depending on the type of the licensed product sold. There is some reason to be wary of a manufacturer's claim of high inventory toward the end of a license term, especially if the products have been selling well all along. Inflating inventory may be a disguised attempt to extend the terms of the license.

14. Purchase at Cost

A. Licensor shall have the right to purchase from Licensee, at Licensee's manufacturing cost, such number of Licensed Products as Licensor may specify in writing to Licensee, but not to exceed one gross for any Licensed Product. For purposes of this Paragraph, "manufacturing cost" shall be $3.75 per Licensed Product. Any amounts due to Licensee pursuant to this Paragraph shall not be deducted from any royalties, including any minimum royalties, owed to Licensor.

B. Licensee agrees to give the Licensor, without charge, twelve each of the Licensed Products.

These two provisions provide a way for the designer to obtain samples of the licensed products for personal use and promotion. It is not intended to provide the licensor with a source of goods for sale in competition with the licensee. Some licensees are very wary of allowing an unlimited purchase right and will specify a limit.

15. Miscellaneous Provisions

A. Nothing herein shall be construed to constitute the parties hereto partners or joint venturers, nor shall any similar relationship be deemed to exist between them.

This provision states that the relationship between the parties is not a partnership or joint venture (which is a form of partnership). Being a member of a partnership has significant tax and legal consequences, such as liability of one partner for the acts of another partner. Partners can bind the partnership to other agreements. The relationship between licensee and licensor is almost always an independent relationship, with the artist or designer acting as an independent contractor.

B. The rights herein granted are personal to the Licensee and shall not be transferred or assigned, in whole or in part, without the prior written consent of the Licensor.

It is standard procedure to prohibit the licensee from assigning its rights or transferring its obligations under a license to another. An example of a sublicense would be a situation in which the licensee subcontracts with a third party to produce the licensed product. The reason for barring such an action is control. By selecting one licensee over another, the artist has determined (or should have determined) that the licensee will produce and sell a high-quality product. If the licensee assigns its rights to another company, unknown to the artist, the ability to control the quality of the licensed product is diminished.

If the designer does not care particularly about who produces the licensed articles, but only wants to know the identity of the third party, a provision such as the following would be acceptable:

Licensee shall not have a third party manufacture or produce the Licensed Product without the Licensor's prior written consent.

If this were the only limitation, notice that the licensee might be free to have others distribute and sell the licensed products and would not need the licensor's consent. This result may not have been intended by the licensor. A better practice would be to use the provision in the paragraph under analysis, and carve out an exception, rather than give blanket consent.

In the absence of a specific provision allowing assignments and sublicensing, most courts will treat a license agreement as one personal to the licensee and prevent the licensee from assigning its obligations to a third party. It is better to include a provision like this one than to have to commence a lawsuit to try to achieve the same result.

C. No waiver of any condition or covenant of this Agreement by either party hereto shall be deemed to imply or constitute a further waiver by such party of the same or any other condition. This Agreement shall be binding upon and shall inure to the benefit of the parties, their successors, and assigns.

This waiver provision is intended to guard against a defaulting party's claim that, because a prior default was ignored by the other party, the injured party has lost its right to challenge a subsequent default. For example, the licensor's approval copy of a product is received a week late and the licensor does not take any action. Later, an approval is skipped. The licensee might argue that the licensor's right to demand compliance with subsequent approvals was waived by its failure to take action in the previous matter. This provision negates such an argument.

D. Whatever claim Licensor may have against Licensee hereunder for royalties or for damages shall become a first lien upon all of the items produced under this Agreement in the possession or under the control of the Licensee upon the expiration or termination of this Agreement.

A lien is a charge upon specific property to secure payment or discharge of a particular debt or duty. This contract provision creates a lien on inventory in the possession or control of the licensee as a means to secure the payment of any outstanding royalties or damages sustained.

E. This Agreement shall be construed in accordance with the laws of New York. The Licensee hereby consents to submit to the personal jurisdiction of the Supreme Court, New York County, and Federal Court of the Southern District of New York for all purposes in connection with this Agreement.

The choice of law governing the agreement should not be overlooked. Although the tendency is to select the law that governs the location of the licensor, there can be countervailing factors which recommend choice of another state's law. For instance, states like California and New York have well-developed bodies of commercial and contract law with considerable legal precedent on the subject of licensing. The judiciary is used to dealing with licensing cases. Typically, the juries in states like these are more sophisticated and more likely to understand and appreciate the value of the artist's or designer's work and consequently award damages which reflect this understanding.

F. All notices and demands shall be sent in writing by certified mail, return receipt requested, at the addresses above first written; royalty statements, payments, and samples of Licensed Products and related materials shall be sent by regular mail.

The notice provision helps avoid confusion as to where and to whom notice should be sent. The writing requirement eliminates claims by one party that it did not receive notice when such notice was given orally by the other.

G. This Agreement constitutes the entire agreement between the parties hereto and shall not be modified, amended or changed in any way except by a written agreement signed by both parties hereto.

This paragraph is known as an integration provision. Its intended purpose is make sure that the parties understand that only the terms and conditions as set forth in the contract are the terms and conditions of their agreement. The effect of this provision means that any prior discussions, representations, letters of intent, and other notes and memoranda which may contain terms and conditions at variance with those in the final agreement have been superseded by those of the final agreement. It precludes the introduction of any prior or contemporaneous agreements as well as oral discussions. All changes or modifications to the agreement must be in writing and signed by both parties, again to preclude changes which were not agreed upon by both parties. Note how designs added to the "Designs" in Schedule B to the agreement must be initialed by both parties.

IN WITNESS WHEREOF, the parties have executed this Licensing Agreement on the date first set forth above.

————————————————————
LICENSEE (COMPANY NAME)

BY:_____
(NAME, POSITION)

————————————————————
SALLY STEVENS, LICENSOR

Two copies of the agreement should be signed and dated by the licensor and licensee or by authorized individuals representing the licensee and licensor, if the parties are not individuals but corporations or partnerships. All changes to the typed agreement should be initialed by each party. The agreement, to be effective, need not be notarized.

Licensing Agreement Between Sally Stevens
and Geoart Inc., dated May 1, 1990

SCHEDULE A.

1. List and Description of Designs

> Beans by the Sea
> Apples by the Sea
> Jazz by the Sea
> Trolleys by the Sea
> Stars by the Sea

Licensee is obligated to inform Licensor in writing at such time
that Licensee abandons a Design, whereupon all rights in and
to the Design shall revert immediately to the Licensor. Additions
to this List made after this Agreement is signed must be added
to the annexed Schedule B and initialed by both Licensor and
Licensee.

Sometimes a particular design does not sell well (through
no fault of the licensee) and the licensee wishes to drop it from
the collection. Rather than leave the design to an uncertain
future, this provision releases the licensee from further obligations concerning the design in exchange for the immediate
reversion of the design rights to the licensor. The licensor is
then free to re-license the design to others.

2. Term of License

Two (2) years commencing June 1, 1990 and ending May 31,
1992. On the condition that the Licensee is not in default of any
term or condition of this Agreement, including all payments
required by Paragraphs 3 and 4 of this Agreement, the Licensee may renew this License for an additional two (2) year term
by written notice to the Licensor given ninety (90) days prior to
the end of the term hereof.

Settling on the initial license term is often the subject of extensive negotiations. A variety of factors come into play which affect the length of time. The strength of the licensee's business reputation in its particular market niche is a major consideration. So, too, is the licensee's particular history with handling the kind of designs being offered and the type of products being licensed.

There is no "standard" license term. Too long a term can lock a designer into a "bad" deal which might cause the designer to miss other, worthier opportunities. Too short a term may discourage a possible licensee from investing in the work because, based on a cost benefit analysis, the term may not be long enough to allow the licensee to recoup the expenses of royalties, advances, and costs of producing the licensed items. The offer of a long-term agreement, especially made as part of the initial offer, can be an indication of the licensee's confidence in the design or the designer.

What, then, is an appropriate term for a licensing agreement? A company with a proven track record or with strong market capabilities is a better risk for a longer arrangement than a newcomer, especially if the royalty rate and advance are set at acceptable levels. However, be wary of granting a long term license to a novice licensee. Improper marketing, due to lack of experience, can destroy the image. In these circumstances, a one-year term with the option to renew the term up to two one-year terms may present an acceptable compromise. The licensee would then be willing to make the necessary investment in the designs and rely on the fact that, if the products were successful, the one-year term could be rolled over into a three-year term.

What is the useful life of the design itself? The character Eloise is as strong a character today as she was in 1956 when she was created. Compare this with the waning popularity for Cabbage Patch Dolls over the past few years since their introduction. A strong design with broad public recognition justifies a longer term.

The nature of the work licensed also may dictate the length of the term. For example, a really "hot" product design—or the product which embodies it—might be knocked-off or imitated soon after it debuts. Sales for the first month could be extraordinary—before imitators cut into market share. So, here, the length of term would not be as important as the need to protect royalties (see prior discussion on royalties, paragraphs 3 and 4 of the Agreement) and receive as large an advance as possible.

It is not unusual for a licensee to want to extend the term of a license beyond the initial period. An artist can expect to have to bargain over this right. Keep in mind that for this additional right (or for any additional right), the *quid pro quo* of negotiation calls for the receipt of a benefit of some kind.

It is appropriate to make the right to extend the initial term of the license conditional upon the licensee's being in full compliance with the license terms at the time the extension is requested. The right to extend the term should not be exercisable unless the licensee is current in the payment of all royalties and minimum guarantees, if any. In addition, the licensor might want to stipulate that other criteria be fulfilled; for example, that products sold or actual royalties (not advances or guaranteed royalties) have to exceed minimum figures to allow the right to be exercised. Of course, the option to extend the term can be drafted to require the payment of an increased royalty rate or higher guaranteed royalties during the renewal period.

3. Territory

Beans by the Sea - Boston, Massachusetts only

Apples by the Sea - New York, New York only

Jazz by the Sea - New Orleans, Louisiana only

Trolleys by the Sea - San Francisco, California only

Stars by the Sea - Los Angeles, California only

The geographical area in which sales for the licensed properties will be permitted should be clearly stipulated, primarily to avoid the granting of overlapping licenses. If sales in the United States only are intended, do not agree to "North America" which includes Canada and Mexico, or, for example, do not use "Europe," which may include Eastern as well as Western Europe, when only France, Italy, and Switzerland are intended.

4. Licensed Products

The Products on which the Licensee is permitted to use the Designs are:

T-Shirts	Coffee Mugs
Postcards	Tote Bags

Licensee may use the Designs on other articles provided the Licensee obtains the Licensor's prior written consent, which Licensor agrees not to withhold unreasonably, and provided that a mutually satisfactory royalty is agreed upon as a condition of obtaining consent.

It is advisable to build flexibility into a licensing agreement to allow expansion for a successful licensing campaign. It is not uncommon for a licensee to want to expand the product line even during the initial term of the agreement if the designs are selling well. Rather than go through the time and legal expense of negotiating another agreement, the initial agreement can be tailored to accommodate this prospect through the incorporation of a provision like this one. Of course, thought should be given to whether the licensee is competent to handle the added product line.

5. Production Schedule

Licensee shall commence production of the Licensed Products on or about: July 15, 1990; and Licensed Products shall be introduced for sale on the market on or about: September 1, 1990.

The overall plan for the commercial exploitation of the products should be known before the licensor signs on the dotted line. The date the products are to be introduced for sale is critical, especially if the product or design is season- or holiday-oriented. The nature and scope of the advertising and promotional campaign, if any, should be discussed ahead of time. It is desirable to specify the advertising or promotional efforts the licensee is going to undertake. For example, the licensor may want to require the licensee to attend specific trade shows to distribute brochures and other materials which promote the designer and the designer's work.

6. Design and Production Services

Licensor will provide art in the form of a line drawing accompanied by a color sketch. If camera-ready art is to be furnished, all original art work shall be returned to Licensor within sixty (60) days after manufacturing of approved samples of each of the Licensed Products. Licensee shall be solely responsible for all risks, damage, and loss of the artwork while in its possession or in transportation from Licensee to Licensor.

Licensee shall reimburse Licensor for any camera-ready art preparations (mechanicals and color separations) and expenses incurred in furnishing camera-ready art to Licensee for the manufacture of the Licensed Products. Art preparation expenses will also include, without limitation, special supplies such as typography required to be set, photostats, transparencies, and film positives.

Since the creation of artwork is necessary, the costs of producing the artwork must be allocated between licensor and licensee. Also, when the artwork is not delivered in finished form and the licensee finalizes the artwork, there is some risk that the licensee may claim ownership rights in the final artwork. See the "work made for hire" issues addressed in chapter 2. Accordingly, the artist or designer should always reserve the right to approve the final artwork (see Schedule B) and include a sentence stating:

All artwork created under the Agreement, regardless of who prepared it or worked on it, is owned by the Licensor.

7. Production and Related Expenses

The following costs relating to this License shall be paid by the Licensee: costs of travel and lodging incurred for personal appearances and tours by the Licensor.

Initials: _____   _____

               LICENSOR'S   LICENSEE'S

Dated: _____

This provision should list any unusual production costs or expenses incurred by the licensor in connection with the license. The entire Schedule A should be initialed by both parties upon execution of the agreement.

Licensing Agreement Between Sally Stevens and Geoart Inc., dated May 1, 1990

SCHEDULE B.

LIST AND DESCRIPTION OF ADDITIONAL DESIGNS

_____   _____

_____   _____

_____   _____

_____   _____

Initials: _____   _____
               LICENSOR'S   LICENSEE'S

Dated: _____

      Schedule B is included so that other designs can be added and become subject to the terms of this licensing agreement. This procedure is recommended when the terms and conditions affecting the new designs are the same as those for the existing designs. Each time a new design(s) is added, another schedule should be completed and signed in duplicate, with each party attaching a copy to the agreement.

Licensing Agreement Between Sally Stevens and Geoart Inc., dated May 1, 1990

SCHEDULE C.

APPROVAL SCHEDULE

LICENSEE:_____

DESIGN:_____

LICENSED PRODUCT:_____

SUBMISSION DATE:	STAGE	LICENSOR'S APPROVAL INITIALS AND DATE
	Variations from Submitted Preliminary Design/Prototype	
	Mechanicals or Camera-Ready Art	
	Production Sample	
	Revised Production Sample	
	Final Design	

This schedule should be adapted to meet the needs of the particular manufacturing process or the type of artwork submitted. It is intended as a checklist to help the artist and designer keep tabs on the production and quality control requirements of the license.

Chapter 5

The Model Licensing Agreements

T he Model Long Form Licensing Agreement conforms to the agreement previously discussed at length in the prior chapter. The Model Short Form Agreement is an abridged version of the long form agreement with the long form's key terms and conditions embodied in a simpler format. The long form's schedules are omitted in the short form, as are many of the definitional paragraphs to make the agreement appear "simpler." It is suggested that this agreement be used in those instances when the license is for a single image for a single use (for example, a design for a bathroom shower curtain) or when the designer or artist justifiably believes the licensee will be put off by the long form. In almost all instances, the long form is the recommended version and should be used with modifications if necessary.

The Checklist for Negotiating Licensing Agreements can be used as a helpful summary to review the numerous points that should be discussed when negotiating a proposed agreement. It tracks the Model Long Form Agreement and should be referred to when reading through any proposed agreement.

MODEL LONG FORM LICENSING AGREEMENT

1. Grant of License

AGREEMENT MADE this ___ day of _____, 19__ between
_____, having an address at _____
_____, (the "Licensor") and _____, lo-
cated at _____, (the "Licensee") whereby Licensor
grants to Licensee a license to use the designs listed on the attached
Schedules A and B (the "Designs") in accordance with the terms and
conditions of this Agreement and only for the production, sale, advertising, and promotion of certain articles (the "Licensed Products") described in Schedule A for the Term and in the Territory set forth in said
Schedule. Licensee shall have the right to affix the Trademarks:
_____ and _____ on or to the Licensed Products and on
packaging, advertising, and promotional materials sold, used, or distributed in connection with the Licensed Products.

2. Licensor's Representation and Credits

A. Licensor warrants that Licensor has the right to grant to the Licensee
all of the rights conveyed in this Agreement. The Licensee shall have no
right, license, or permission except as herein expressly granted. All rights
not specifically transferred by this Agreement are reserved to the
Licensor.

B. The Licensee prominently shall display and identify the Licensor as the
designer on each Licensed Product and on all packaging, advertising,
displays and in all publicity therefor and shall have reproduced thereon
(or on an approved tag or label) the following notices: "© Licensor's
name, 19__. All rights reserved." The Licensed Products shall be marketed under the name: _____ for _____. The name
_____ shall not be cojoined with any third party's name without
the Licensor's express written permission.

C. The Licensee shall have the right to use the Licensor's name, portrait, or picture, in a dignified manner consistent with the Licensor's reputation, in advertising or other promotional materials associated with the sale of the Licensed Products.

3. Royalties and Statements of Account

A. Licensee agrees to pay Licensor a nonrefundable royalty of _____ (__%) percent of the net sales of all of the Licensed Products incorporating and embodying the Designs. "Net sales" is defined as sales direct to customers less prepaid freight and credits for lawful and customary volume rebates, actual returns, and allowances; the aggregate of said deductions and credits shall not exceed three (3%) percent of accrued royalties in any year. No costs incurred in the manufacture, sale, distribution, or exploitation of the Licensed Products shall be deducted from any royalties due to Licensor. Royalties shall be deemed to accrue when the Licensed Products are sold, shipped, or invoiced, whichever first occurs.

B. Royalty payments for all sales shall be due on the 15th day after the end of each calendar quarter. At that time and regardless if any Licensed Products were sold during the preceding time period, Licensee shall furnish Licensor an itemized statement categorized by Design, showing the kinds and quantities of all Licensed Products sold and the prices received therefor, and all deductions for freight, volume rebates, returns, and allowances. The first royalty statement shall commence on: _____, 19__.

C. If Licensor has not received the royalty payment as required by the foregoing paragraph 3B within 21 days following the end of each calendar quarter, a monthly service charge of one-and-a-half (1.5%) percent shall accrue thereon and become due and owing from the date on which such royalty payment became due and owing.

4. Advances and Minimum Royalties

A. In each year of this Agreement, Licensee agrees to pay Licensor a Guaranteed Minimum Royalty in the amount of $_____ of which $_____ shall be deemed a Nonrefundable Advance against royalties. The difference, if any, between the Advance and the Guaranteed Minimum Royalty shall be divided equally and paid quarterly over the term of this Agreement commencing with the quarter beginning _____, 19__.

B. The Nonrefundable Advance shall be paid on the signing of this Agreement. No part of the Guaranteed Minimum Royalty or the Nonrefundable Advance shall be repayable to Licensee.

C. On signing of this Agreement, Licensee shall pay Licensor a nonrefundable design fee in the amount of $_____ per Design. This fee shall not be applied against royalties.

D. Licensor has the right to terminate this Agreement upon the giving of thirty (30) days' notice to Licensee if the Licensee fails to pay any portion of the Guaranteed Minimum Royalty when due.

5. Books and Records

Licensee agrees to keep complete and accurate books and records relating to the sale and other distribution of each of the Licensed Products. Licensor or its representative shall have the right to inspect Licensee's books and records relating to the sales of the Licensed Products upon thirty (30) days prior written notice. Any discrepancies over 5% between the royalties received and the royalties due will be subject to the royalty payment set forth herein and paid immediately. If the audit discloses such an underpayment of 10% or more, Licensee shall reimburse the Licensor for all the costs of said audit.

6. Quality of Licensed Products, Approval, and Advertising

A. Licensee agrees that the Licensed Products shall be of the highest standard and quality and of such style and appearance as to be best suited to their exploitation to the best advantage and to the protection and enhancement of the Licensed Products and the good will pertaining thereto. The Licensed Products shall be manufactured, sold, and distributed in accordance with all applicable national, state, and local laws.

B. In order to insure that the development, manufacture, appearance, quality, and distribution of each Licensed Product is consonant with the Licensor's good will associated with its reputation, copyrights, and trademarks, Licensor shall have the right to approve in advance the quality of the Licensed Products (including, without limitation, concepts and preliminary prototypes, mechanicals, or camera-ready art prior to production of first sample; production sample and revised production sample, if any) and all packaging, advertising, literature, publicity, promotion, and displays for the Licensed Products.

C. Licensee shall be responsible for delivering all items requiring prior approval pursuant to Paragraph 6B without cost to the Licensor. Licensor agrees not to withhold approval unreasonably.

D. Licensee shall not release or distribute any Licensed Product without securing each of the prior approvals provided for in Paragraph 6B. Licensee shall not depart from any approval secured in accordance with Paragraph 6B without Licensor's prior written consent.

E. Licensee agrees to expend at least ____% percent of anticipated gross sales of the Licensed Products annually to promote and advertise sales of the Licensed Products.

7. Nonexclusive Rights

Nothing in this Agreement shall be construed to prevent Licensor from granting other licenses for the use of the Designs or from utilizing the Designs in any manner whatsoever, except that the Licensor shall not grant other Licenses for the use of the Designs in connection with the sale of the Licensed Products in the Territory to which this License extends during the term of this Agreement.

8. Nonacquisition of Rights

The Licensee's use of the Designs and Trademarks shall inure to the benefit of the Licensor. If Licensee acquires any trade rights, trademarks, equities, titles, or other rights in and to the Designs or in the Trademark, by operation of law, usage, or otherwise during the term of this Agreement or any extension thereof, Licensee shall forthwith upon the expiration of this Agreement or any extension thereof or sooner termination, assign and transfer the same to Licensor without any consideration other than the consideration of this Agreement.

9. Licensee's Representations

The Licensee warrants and represents that during the term of this License and for any time thereafter, it, or any of its affiliated, associated, or subsidiary companies will not copy, imitate, or authorize the imitation or copying of the Designs, Tradenames, and Trademarks, or any distinctive feature of the foregoing or other designs submitted to the Licensee by Licensor. Without prejudice to any other remedies the Licensor may have, royalties as provided herein shall accrue and be paid by Licensee on all items embodying and incorporating imitated or copied Designs.

10. Registrations and Infringements

A. The Licensor has the right but not the obligation to obtain at its own cost appropriate copyright, trademark, and patent protection for the Designs and the Trademarks. At Licensor's request and at Licensee's sole cost and expense, Licensee shall make all necessary and appropriate registrations to protect the copyrights, trademarks, and patents in and to the Licensed Products and the advertising, promotional, and packaging material in the Territory in which the Licensed Products are sold. Copies of all applications shall be submitted for approval to Licensor prior to filing. The Licensee and Licensor agree to cooperate with each other to assist in the filing of said registrations.

B. Licensee shall not at any time apply for or abet any third party to apply for copyright, trademark, or patent protection which would affect Licensor's ownership of any rights in the Designs or the Trademarks.

C. Licensee shall notify Licensor in writing immediately upon discovery of any infringements or imitations by others of the Designs, Tradenames, or Trademarks. Licensor in its sole discretion may bring any suit, action, or proceeding Licensor deems appropriate to protect Licensor's rights in the Designs, Tradenames, and Trademarks, including, without limitation, for copyright and trademark infringement and for unfair competition.

   If for any reason, Licensor does not institute any such suit or take any such action or proceeding, upon written notice to the Licensee, Licensee may institute such appropriate suit, action, or proceeding in Licensee's and Licensor's names. In any event, Licensee and Licensor shall cooperate fully with each other in the prosecution of such suit, action, or proceeding. Licensor reserves the right, at Licensor's cost and expense, to join in any pending suit, action, or proceeding.

The instituting party shall pay all costs and expenses, including legal fees, incurred by the instituting party. All recoveries and awards, including settlements received, after payments of costs and legal fees, shall be divided seventy-five (75%) percent to the instituting party and twenty-five (25%) percent to the other party.

11. Indemnification and Insurance

A. The Licensee hereby agrees to indemnify and hold the Licensor harmless against all liability, cost, loss, expense (including reasonable attorney's fees), or damages paid, incurred, or occasioned by any claim, demand, suit, settlement, or recovery against the Licensor, without limitation, arising out of the breach or claim of breach of this Agreement; the use of the Designs by it or any third party; the manufacture, distribution, and sale of the Licensed Products; and for any alleged defects in the Licensed Products. Licensee hereby consents to submit to the personal jurisdiction of any court, tribunal, or forum in which an action or proceeding is brought involving a claim to which this foregoing indemnification shall apply.

B. Licensee shall obtain at its sole cost and expense product liability insurance in an amount providing sufficient and adequate coverage, but not less than $1,000,000 combined single limit coverage protecting the Licensor against any claims or lawsuits arising from alleged defects in the Licensed Product.

12. Grounds for and Consequences of Termination

A. Licensor shall have the right to terminate this Agreement by written notice, and all the rights granted to the Licensee shall revert forthwith to the Licensor and all royalties or other payments shall become due and payable immediately if:

i. Licensee fails to comply with or fulfill any of the terms or conditions of this Agreement;

ii. the Licensed Products have not been offered or made available for sale by Licensee _____ (____) months from the date hereof;

iii. Licensee ceases to manufacture and sell the Licensed Products in commercially reasonable quantities; or

iv. the Licensee is adjudicated a bankrupt, makes an assignment for the benefit of creditors, or liquidates its business.

B. Licensee, as quickly as possible, but in no event later than thirty (30) days after such termination, shall submit to Licensor the statements required in Paragraph 3 for all sales and distributions through the date of termination. Licensor shall have the right to conduct an actual inventory on the date of termination or thereafter to verify the accuracy of said statements.

C. In the event of termination all payments theretofore made to the Licensor shall belong to the Licensor without prejudice to any other remedies the Licensor may have.

13. Sell-off Right

Provided Licensee is not in default of any term or condition of this Agreement, Licensee shall have the right for a period of _____ (____) months from the expiration of this Agreement or any extension thereof to sell inventory on hand subject to the terms and conditions of this Agreement, including the payment of royalties and guaranteed minimum royalties on sales which continue during this additional period.

14. Purchase at Cost

A. Licensor shall have the right to purchase from Licensee, at Licensee's manufacturing cost, such number of Licensed Products as Licensor may specify in writing to Licensee, but not to exceed _____ (____) for any Licensed Product. For purposes of this Paragraph, "manufacturing cost" shall mean $_____ per Licensed Product. Any amounts due to Licensee pursuant to this Paragraph shall not be deducted from any royalties, including any minimum royalties, owed to Licensor.

B. Licensee agrees to give the Licensor, without charge, _____ (_____) each of the Licensed Products.

15. Miscellaneous Provisions

A. Nothing herein shall be construed to constitute the parties hereto partners or joint venturers, nor shall any similar relationship be deemed to exist between them.

B. The rights herein granted are personal to the Licensee and shall not be transferred or assigned, in whole or in part, without the prior written consent of the Licensor.

C. No waiver of any condition or covenant of this Agreement by either party hereto shall be deemed to imply or constitute a further waiver by such party of the same or any other condition. This Agreement shall be binding upon and shall inure to the benefit of the parties, their successors, and assigns.

D. Whatever claim Licensor may have against Licensee hereunder for royalties or for damages shall become a first lien upon all of the items produced under this Agreement in the possession or under the control of the Licensee upon the expiration or termination of this Agreement.

E. This Agreement shall be construed in accordance with the laws of _____. The Licensee hereby consents to submit to the personal jurisdiction of the _____Court, _____ County, and Federal Court of the _____ District of _____ for all purposes in connection with this Agreement.

F. All notices and demands shall be sent in writing by certified mail, return receipt requested, at the addresses above first written; royalty statements, payments, and samples of Licensed Products and related materials shall be sent by regular mail.

G. This Agreement constitutes the entire agreement between the parties hereto and shall not be modified, amended, or changed in any way except by written agreement signed by both parties hereto. Licensee shall not assign this Agreement.

IN WITNESS WHEREOF, the parties have executed this Licensing Agreement on the date first set forth above.

_____
LICENSEE (COMPANY NAME)

BY:_____
(NAME, POSITION)

_____
LICENSOR

Licensing Agreement Between

_____ and _____,

Dated _____, 19__.

SCHEDULE A.

1. List and Description of Designs

_____ _____

_____ _____

_____ _____

Licensee is obligated to inform Licensor in writing at such time that Licensee abandons a Design, whereupon all rights in and to the Design shall revert immediately to the Licensor. Additions to this List made after this Agreement is signed must be added to the annexed Schedule B and initialed by both Licensor and Licensee.

2. Term of License

_____ (_____) years commencing _____, 19__ and ending _____, 19__. On the condition that the Licensee is not in default of any term or condition of this Agreement, including all payments required by Paragraphs 3 and 4 of this Agreement, the Licensee may renew this License for an additional _____ (_____) year term by written notice to the Licensor given ninety (90) days prior to the end of the term hereof.

3. Territory

_____

_____

4. Licensed Products

The Products on which the Licensee is permitted to use the Designs are:

_____ _____

_____ _____

_____ _____

Licensee may use the Designs on other articles provided that Licensee obtains the prior written consent of the Licensor, which Licensor shall not withhold unreasonably, and provided that a mutually satisfactory royalty is agreed upon as a condition of obtaining consent.

5. Production Schedule

Licensee shall commence production of the Licensed Products on or about: _____, 19__; and Licensed Products shall be introduced for sale on the market on or about: _____, 19 __ .

6. Design and Production Services

Licensor will provide art in the form of:

_____

_____

All original artwork shall be returned to Licensor within sixty (60) days after manufacturing of approved samples of each of the Licensed Products. Licensee shall be solely responsible for all risks, damage, and loss of the artwork while in its possession or in transportation from Licensee to Licensor.

Licensee shall reimburse Licensor for any camera-ready art preparations (mechanical color separations) and expenses incurred in furnishing camera-ready art to Licensee for the manufacture of the Licensed Products. Art preparation expenses will also include, without limitation, special supplies such as typography required to be set, photostats, transparencies, and film positives.

7. Related Expenses

The following costs related to the Licensed Products shall be paid by the Licensee:

_____	_____
_____	_____
_____	_____

Initials: _____   _____

                        LICENSOR'S   LICENSEE'S

Licensing Agreement Between

_____ and _____

Dated _____, 19__.

SCHEDULE B.

LIST AND DESCRIPTION OF ADDITIONAL DESIGNS:

_____   _____

_____   _____

_____   _____

_____   _____

Initials: _____   _____
               LICENSOR'S   LICENSEE'S

Date:_____

Licensing Agreement Between

_____ and _____,

Dated _____, 19__.

SCHEDULE C.
APPROVAL SCHEDULE

LICENSEE:_____

DESIGN:_____

LICENSED PRODUCT:_____

SUBMISSION DATE:	STAGE	LICENSOR'S APPROVAL INITIALS AND DATE
	Variations from Submitted Preliminary Design/Prototype	
	Mechanicals or Camera-Ready Art	
	Production Sample	
	Revised Production Sample	
	Final Design	

MODEL SHORT FORM LICENSING AGREEMENT

1._____(the "Licensor") hereby grants to
_____(the "Licensee") a non-
exclusive license to use the _____image (the "Image")
created and owned by Licensor on _____ ("Licensed
Products") and to distribute and sell these Licensed Products in
_____ for a term of _____ (__) years commencing
_____, 19____, in accordance with the terms and conditions of
this Agreement.

2. Licensor shall retain all copyrights in and to the Image. The Licensee
shall identify the Licensor as the artist on the Licensed Products and shall
reproduce thereon the following copyright notice: "© Licensor's name
19___."

3. Licensee agrees to pay Licensor a nonrefundable royalty of _____
(____%) percent of the net sales of the Licensed Products. "Net Sales"
as used herein shall mean sales to customers less prepaid freight and
credits for lawful and customary volume rebates, actual returns, and
allowances. Royalties shall be deemed to accrue when the Licensed
Products are sold, shipped, or invoiced, whichever first occurs.

4. Licensee shall pay Licensor a nonrefundable advance in the amount
of $_____ upon signing of this Agreement. Licensee further agrees to
pay Licensor a guaranteed nonrefundable minimum royalty of
$_____ every month.

5. Royalty payments shall be paid on the first day of each month
commencing _____, 19__, and Licensee shall furnish Licensor with
monthly statements of account showing the kinds and quantities of all
Licensed Products sold, the prices received therefor, and all deductions
for freight, volume rebates, returns, and allowances. The first royalty
statement shall be sent on _____, 19__.

6. Licensor shall have the right to terminate this Agreement upon thirty (30) days notice if Licensee fails to make any payment required of it and does not cure this default within said thirty (30) days, whereupon all rights granted herein shall revert immediately to the Licensor.

7. Licensee agrees to keep complete and accurate books and records relating to the sale of the Licensed Products. Licensor shall have the right to inspect Licensee's books and records concerning sales of the Licensed Products upon prior written notice.

8. Licensee shall give Licensor free of charge _____ samples of each of the Licensed Products for Licensor's personal use. Licensor shall have the right to purchase additional samples of the Licensed Products at the Licensee's manufacturing cost. "Manufacturing cost" shall be $____ per Licensed Product.

9. Licensor shall have the right to approve the quality of the reproduction of the Image on the Licensed Products and on any approved advertising or promotional materials and Licensor shall not unreasonably withhold approval.

10. Licensee shall use its best efforts to promote, distribute, and sell the Licensed Products and said Products shall be of the highest commercial quality.

11. All rights not specifically transferred by this Agreement are reserved to the Licensor.

12. The Licensee shall hold the Licensor harmless from and against any loss, expense, or damage occasioned by any claim, demand, suit, or recovery against the Licensor arising out of the use of the Image.

13. Nothing herein shall be construed to constitute the parties hereto joint venturers, nor shall any similar relationship be deemed to exist between them. This Agreement shall not be assigned in whole or in part without the prior written consent of the Licensor.

14. This Agreement shall be construed in accordance with the laws of
_____; Licensee consents to jurisdiction of the courts of _____.

15. All notices, demands, payments, royalty payments and statements
shall be sent to the Licensor at the following address:
_____; and to the Licensee at:
_____.

16. This Agreement constitutes the entire agreement between the
parties hereto and shall not be modified, amended, or changed in any
way except by written agreement signed by both parties hereto. This
Agreement shall be binding upon and shall inure to the benefit of the
parties, their successors, and assigns.

IN WITNESS WHEREOF, the parties have executed this Licensing Agreement on the _____ day of _____, 19____.

_____
LICENSOR

_____
LICENSEE

By:_____
(Position)

CHECKLIST FOR NEGOTIATING LICENSING AGREEMENTS

- Carefully describe the image to be licensed.

- State whether the rights given to the licensee are exclusive or nonexclusive.

- Indicate for which kinds of merchandise the image is being licensed.

- State the territory in which the licensee may sell the licensed products.

- Give a term for the licensing contract.

- Reserve all copyrights in the image to the artist.

- Require that credit and copyright notice in the artist's name appear on all licensed products.

- Require that credit and copyright notice in the artist's name appear on packaging, advertising, displays, and all publicity.

- Have the right to approve packaging, advertising, displays, and publicity.

- Give the licensee the right to use the artist's name and, in an appropriate case, the artist's picture, provided that any use must be to promote the product and that any presentation of the image must be displayed in a dignified manner.

- Determine whether the royalty should be based on retail price or, as is more commonly the case, on net sales price.

- If any expenses are to reduce the amount on which royalties are calculated, these expenses must be specified.

- Specify the royalty percentage.

- Require the licensee to pay an advance against royalties to be earned.

- Indicate that any advance is nonrefundable.

- Require minimum guaranteed royalty payments for the term of the contract, regardless of sales.

- Require monthly or quarterly statements of account accompanied by any payments which are due.

- Specify the information to be contained in the statement of account, such as units sold, total revenues received, special discounts, and the like.

- Enable the artist to inspect the books and records of the licensee.

- Provide that if an inspection of the books and records uncovers an error to the disadvantage of the artist and that error is more than 10 percent of the amount owed artist, then the licensee shall pay for the cost of the inspection and any related costs.

- Provide for a certain number of samples to be given free to the artist by the manufacturer.

- Give the artist a right to purchase additional samples at manufacturing cost or, at least, at no more than the price paid by wholesalers.

- Consider, if appropriate, whether the artist will want the right to sell the products at retail price, rather than being restricted to using the samples and other units purchased for personal use.

- Give the artist a right of approval over the quality of the reproductions to protect the artist's reputation.

- Require the licensee to use best efforts in promoting the licensed products.

- Specify the amount of money which the licensee must spend on promotion.

- Reserve all rights to the artist which are not expressly transferred to the licensee.

- Require the licensee to indemnify the artist for any costs arising out of the improper use of the image on the licensed products.

- Have the licensee provide liability insurance with the artist as named beneficiary to protect against defects in the licensed products.

- Specify the grounds for terminating the contract, such as the bankruptcy or insolvency of the licensee, failure of the licensee to obey the terms of the contract, cessation of manufacture of the product, or insufficient sales of the licensed products.

This checklist is adapted from that appearing in *Business and Legal Forms for Fine Artists* (Allworth Press, distributed by North Light Books) and appears here by courtesy of the author, Tad Crawford.

Chapter 6

Engaging a Licensing Agent

Many artists and designers turn to licensing agents and representatives for help when they lack leads for locating potential licensees or when they need assistance with organizing and running a licensing program.

A licensing agent should be selected on the basis of his or her ability to generate contracts in the market that the artist wishes to pursue with the particular property to be licensed. An agent's reputation and credentials should be scrutinized carefully. This can be done rather simply. Ask the prospective agent for references and for the names of some past and present clients; then speak with some. Find out about the agent's reputation; ask about his or her success rate with negotiating lucrative or high-profile licenses. Do not be shy or hesitant in asking about the agent's fee or negative points or problems that may have arisen during the course of prior representations.

Be aware that agents usually are specialized and choose to represent only a certain genre of artist or designer (such as a packaging designer or book illustrator) or type of merchandise (like toys, giftware, or stationery). Most are very selective as to whom they will represent and some, quite rightly, will decline to represent an artist when the artist's work is too similar to and will conflict with the work of an artist already represented by the agent. It is crucial that the correct fit be found.

Role of the Licensing Agent

The role of the licensing agent is to maximize the commercial value of the artist's work and seek the best potential licensee for the property consistent with this objective. This assistance is not without a price. Many licensing agents will charge a fee between 15 and 25 percent of all of the compensation received from the licensing of the property. But the payment may be worth making in order to secure work, especially if the design firm or designer has no contacts among potential licensees. Others may seek a higher fee. Fifteen to twenty-five percent is far more reasonable, but certainly a higher fee may be justified when the agent has a proven track record with good contacts and can facilitate the launching of a successful licensing career.

An arrangement with a licensing agent can be one of two types: the first, when the agent assists the artist and seeks potential licensees; the second, when the licensing agent is authorized to act for the artist and is empowered to negotiate and sign contracts on the artist's behalf.

Under the more common and certainly recommended first form, the agent helps negotiate the terms and conditions of the proposed license, presents the proposal to the artist for approval, and generally oversees the operation of the license, including making sure that the products are produced and payments made as required by the agreement.

In the second form, the agent's agreement empowers the agent to act as the artist's "attorney-in-fact" and take any and all steps on the artist's behalf in connection with a licensing agreement. Such a provision delegates very broad authority to the agent. The effect is to nullify the artist's ability to choose the licensee and select the terms of the agreement. Such an appointment of power means that the agent, not the artist, can negotiate and bind a licensor to a contract without the licensor's prior consent. This type of arrangement should be avoided as it vests far too much power in the hands of the agent.

The Agency Agreement

The relationship between the creator of the licensed property and the licensing firm or representative should be governed by an agency agreement. These agreements almost always should be in writing. The designer who wishes to make an agreement with a licensing agent should seek professional legal advice to make sure that the terms of representation are understood.

The "Model Agency Agreement" included at the end of this chapter offers a suggested form. As with all such forms, the artist or designer should adapt its provisions to match the exigencies of the specific arrangement.

Designers should take care to specify the type of work and clients covered and to guard against overly broad agreements and ones that create an exclusive relationship between agent and designer. Such contracts may prove to be too constrictive in the future, as the designer becomes successful and is able to market the work directly.

Other points to be covered in a licensing agent's agreement include the scope of the representation (whether it is exclusive or nonexclusive), term, territory, fees, reservation of house accounts, and a clear definition of the agent's responsibilities.

To elaborate briefly on some of the above points: as to the term, one must understand that the shortest period of time an agent usually is willing to commit to is two years. This is viewed as the minimum start-up time required for an agent's efforts to generate interest in the property. Consider, too, that an agent is unlikely to promote an artist's work or undertake the expense of attending licensing shows if the artist can leave the agent after only a short time. The leads developed during the first year might not ripen into a licensing agreement until after the representation has expired. Unless the agreement gives the agent the right to claim fees for licenses signed as a result of the agent's efforts during the term of the representation, the agent would not receive the benefit of the prior efforts.

It is important to describe the agent's duties carefully. The following language is helpful:

> The agent shall (a) use its best efforts to promote the licensing and exploitation of the artwork in the territory; (b) identify potential licensees and solicit license agreements with such licensees on artist's behalf; (c) provide record keeping and billing services described in the agreement; and (d) supervise the quality of the products developed and sold by licensee.

The contractual relationship, known as "privity of contract," should be established between the artist and the licensee directly, and not between the licensee and agent. Some agent's agreements authorize the agent to seek and obtain its fees from the licensee. This should be avoided. All payments under the agreement should be made to the licensor, who will then remit the agent's share, rather than direct payments from the licensee to the agent. It is important, too, that the artist always be given the right to decline potential agreements.

Who Should Negotiate the Agreement

Should the agent negotiate the terms of the licensing agreement or should an attorney? Because the agent has a direct financial interest in the artist's signing a licensing agreement and receives fees based on a percentage of the payments the artist is to receive (no contract, no fee), an inherent conflict of interest between the agent's desire to be paid a fee for its services and the right of the artist to sign a favorable contract exists. This conflict of interest, if resolved in the agent's favor, could result in the agent's urging the artist to sign a weak contract.

Unlike the higher standard of duty that states such as New York and California impose by law on certain business relationships, like the one between an artist and an art dealer, known as a "fiduciary relationship," no such standard governs the relationship between artist and agent in licensing arrangements.

A "fiduciary" is a person who by law owes a degree of trust to another. By virtue of this status the fiduciary must act primarily for the other's benefit in matters connected with the relationship. It necessitates a higher standard of care and responsibility with regard to the relationship than do ordinary relationships. Conflicts of interest are impermissible. Thus, in the absence of statutory safeguards, it is the responsibility of the licensor to protect against potential conflicts and seek impartial advice.

Lastly, no matter how experienced an agent may be in negotiating the business aspects of a licensing deal, it is the attorney who is trained to analyze the legal implications and to evaluate the risks as well as the merits of the agreement. If appropriate, the attorney will urge an unbiased rejection of the arrangement. For these reasons, it is recommended that an attorney review the licensing agreement, whether procured by the agent or initially offered by the licensee, to ensure that the artist is fully protected.

MODEL AGENCY AGREEMENT

_____

ARTIST/DESIGNER

_____

ADDRESS

_____

AGENT

_____

ADDRESS

DATE:_____

Dear _____:

The following, when signed by you, shall constitute an agreement between us concerning your acting as my agent.

1. I hereby appoint you, and you agree to act, as my licensing agent to promote the designs and images created by me and to secure licensing agreements for the commercial exploitation thereof in the following territory:_____.

2. This agreement shall be for a period of two (2) years from the above date and may be renewed for a one (1) year period upon the same terms and conditions, provided that I give you written notice of my intention to renew at least sixty (60) days prior to expiration of the original term of this agreement.

(or alternatively)

2. This agreement shall be for a period of two (2) years from the above date and may be renewed for a one (1) year period upon the same terms and conditions, provided: I receive gross compensation in excess of $_____ during the initial term of this agreement from license agreements solicited by you and signed by me.

3. You shall use your best efforts to solicit contracts, licensing agreements, and other work for me. All contracts and agreements shall be subject to my prior approval. I reserve the right to reject any proposed work you obtain for me for any reason or no reason at all.

4. During the term of this agreement, your fee shall be fifteen (15%) percent of the gross compensation received by me and I shall make payment to you within ten (10) days of receipt of gross compensation. "Gross compensation" shall mean royalties, design fees, and advances, but shall not include payments for reimbursed expenses incurred by me in connection with the production of my work.

5. You understand and agree that you are not entitled to any fees for any work that I presently am engaged to do or will do for the following accounts,_____

_____

_____,

known as House Accounts, except as otherwise specifically agreed to in writing.

6. You agree to pay all expenses, including but not limited to charges for telephone, postage, faxes, messengers, entertainment, and general business expenses incurred by you in connection with your representation of me.

7. Our relationship shall be that of independent contractors and nothing contained herein shall constitute this arrangement a joint venture or a partnership. You shall not obtain any rights in my work. You also agree to return my work in your possession or under your control (whether in the form of sketches, drawings, or finished artwork) promptly upon my demand.

8. This agreement may be terminated by either of us by giving thirty (30) days prior written notice to the other. If within six (6) months from the date of termination I enter into license agreements with licensees presented by you while this agreement was in effect, you shall be entitled to receive a fee for these agreements, with the fee limited to payments I receive during this six (6) month period, at the same rate as provided above. No fees shall be paid if I terminate this agreement for cause.

9. This agreement is personal to us and shall not be assigned; it shall be binding upon and shall inure to the benefit of our successors, administrators, executors, and heirs.

10. Any claim or controversy arising out of or related to this agreement or the breach thereof shall be settled by arbitration in accordance with the rules of the American Arbitration Association in the City of _____ and State of _____, and the award rendered in such proceedings may be entered in any court having jurisdiction thereof.

11. This agreement shall be governed by and construed in accordance with the laws of the State of _____.

Very truly yours,

_____
Artist/Designer

ACCEPTED AND AGREED:

_____
Agent/Representative

Summing Up

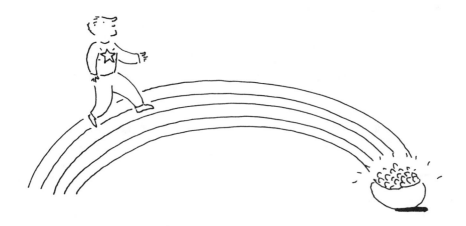

L icensing is about selling a portion of reproduction rights to a work in order to maximize the value of the work. Individual artists and designers as well as design firms can profit handsomely from well-run licensing programs. The licensing fees and royalties generated from these programs can be very lucrative. There is, however, no magic way to achieve this success.

Design professionals who succeed at licensing share certain characteristics. They produce original, creative, quality work and present it professionally. They understand the market for their work and select licensees whose ability to promote and sell products meshes with the work and enhances the work's potential and their reputations. They expand their licensing programs continually by searching out new market sources and buyers devising new applications and uses for existing work. Underscoring all of these points, they are savvy business people who understand licensing well enough to either negotiate their own agreements or know when to retain the services of a professional to do so.

Skillful use of *Licensing Art & Design* can help artists and designers launch a licensing program. The groups and publications mentioned in the Introduction and those listed in the Resouces for Artists and Designers in the Appendices, are good jumping off points to identify prospective licensees. By keeping abreast of developments reported in trade papers, design professionals can identify potential licensees and increase the likelihood of spotting new trends and applications for their work.

Prior to soliciting a license, the artist or designer must know what rights exist in the work. For example, does the artist own the work or can others, such as assistants or employees, claim rights to work? Is the work confusingly or substantially similar to other artists' work so as to make it unwise to attempt to license it? The discussion on copyright and other proprietary rights contained in chapter 2 helps answer these questions.

Before work is presented to an individual or entity who has expressed interest in developing the work commercially and entering into a licensing arrangement, chapter 3's discussion on the protection of artists' and designers' rights in the work against loss through inadvertence or "theft" should be read.

The ability to identify those issues that are important and germane to a potential license is crucial before starting any negotiation. The checklist for negotiating agreements, printed at the end of chapter 5, serves as a handy review of the scope of the licensing process and familiarizes the artist with the major points for negotiation. All of the checklist points are examined in chapter 4's analysis of a typical licensing agreement. The legal and business aspects of each provision are discussed at length.

The pros and cons of the artist's and designer's hiring a licensing agent to locate potential licensees are evaluated in chapter 6. So, too, is the appropriateness of setting limits to the scope of the agent's authority to negotiate licenses and manage the designer's business affairs.

Lastly, the various sample agreements reproduced in the book are intended to serve as guides. Each can be used as a formal contract provided the terms and conditions are modified to reflect existing circumstances.

Appendices

Comparative Average Royalties of Representative Products

PRODUCT TYPE		AVERAGE ROYALTY RATE*
Graphics	Commercial Prints	10-15%
	Posters	10%
	Calendars	5-10%
	Greeting Cards Stationery	2-5%
	Gift Wrap, Plastic Bags	3-5%
	Eurobags	5-8%
	Postcards	3-5%
Apparel	T-shirts	5-10%
	Sweatshirts	5-10%
Household Accessories	Sheets	5-7%
	Towels	4-7%
	Barware	5-7%
	China	3-5%
	Ceramics	3-7%
	Shower Curtains	6-7%
	Blankets	8%
	Mugs	5%
	Tableware	5%
Textiles	Wall Covering	5-10%
	Wallpaper	5-10%
	Fabric	5-10%
	Stitched Art	8-10%
Miscellaneous	Watches	6-8%
	Heat Transfer Patches	6%
	Decals	6-8%
	Hang Tags	6%
	Toys and Games	6-10%

*Based on 1989 wholesale price to customers.

Resources for Artists and Designers

Publications

Accessories Magazine, published monthly by Business Journals, Inc., 50 Day Street, Norwalk, CT 06856, (203) 853-6015, is a trade magazine for manufacturers, designers, and retailers of accessories and apparel.

Accessories Resources, same publisher and address as above, is the National Fashion Accessories Association's guide to the New York accessories market. It not only includes information about its members (listed alphabetically, under product categories), it also contains an international trade show calendar for the current year. A designer could make valuable contacts by attending these events, providing that he or she had first ascertained that the particular trade represented might be interested in the designer's work.

A few of the fairs listed on the calendar are:

The New York International Gift Fair, in January and August, is at the Jacob Javits Center. Contact George Little Management, Inc., 2 Park Avenue, Suite 1100, New York, NY 10016, (212) 686-6070.

The Merchandise Mart in Chicago, with fairs in February and July, handles home accessories. Call the Merchandise Mart at (312) 527-7632.

The Denver Merchandise Mart, with shows in February and August, is for vendors of jewelry. Contact the Merchandise Mart, 451 East 58th Street, Denver, CO 80216, (303) 292-6278, ext. 5295.

The Boston Gift Show, held at the Bayside Exposition Center in Boston, takes place in March and in September. Contact George Little Management, Inc., 2 Park Avenue, Suite 1100, New York, NY 10016, (212) 686-6070.

American Craft, published bimonthly by the American Craft Council, 40 West 53rd Street, New York, NY 10019, (212) 956-3535.This magazine is geared toward craftspeople in all media, as well as toward craft consumers.

Artist's Market, published annually by F & W Publications, North Light Books, 1507 Dana Avenue, Cincinatti, OH 45209, (800) 269-0963, is an encyclopedia of information for commercial artists. It contains articles pertaining to aspects of commercial art, as well as detailed profiles of companies which hire freelancers or job out projects. (The profiles include names and titles of company employees.) The businesses covered are subdivided according to product category.

Business Organizations, Agencies, and Publications Directory, Gale Research Company, Book Tower, Detroit, MI 48226, (313) 961-2242, contains a list of trade fairs in this country and world wide. Since this listing is not limited in scope (it runs the gamut from auto exhibitions to food shows), one would have to spend some time studying it in order to glean useful information. However, the list is subdivided by categories (i.e., giftware, apparel, stationery), and as the information for each entry is quite complete (including names) it could be a source of contacts.

Often, the merchandise marts or marketing centers that run the varous exhibitions publish directories for each show. Ordering such a listing from the show's or convention's producer would be informative as to whether or not vendors of interest to designers or artists were to be represented.

The Crafts Report, 700 Orange Street, Wilmington, DE 19801, (302) 656-4500, is a monthly report dealing with marketing and management for crafts professionals.

Gayer's Dealer Topics, published monthly by Gayer-McAllister Publications, 51 Madison Avenue, New York, NY 10010, (212) 689-4411, focuses on the stationery trade.

Gift and Decorative Accessory Buyers Directory, published once a year by Gayer-McAllister Publications, see address and phone number for previous entry, is for retailers and manufacturers of gifts and accessories.

Gift and Decorative Accessories Magazine, monthly publication from Gayer-McAllister, see phone number and address for the previous entry.

Gift and Stationery Business, Gralla Publications, 1515 Broadway New York, NY 10036, (212) 869-1300, monthly publication for the stationery trade.

Playthings Magazine, monthly publication from Gayer-McAllister Publications, 51 Madison Avenue, New York, NY 10010, (212) 689-4411, is for toy buyers and manufacturers.

Playthings Directory, annual publication from Gayer-McAllister. See address and phone number for previous entry.

Thomas's Registry of American Manufacturers and Thomas's Register Catalogue file, published annually by Thomas Publishing Company, One Penn Plaza, New York, NY 10001, (212) 695-0500. This enormous reference set (comprising 21 volumes) contains much information that falls outside the area of interest of the artist or designer who is looking for business contacts. However, the first 12 volumes, labeled "Products and Services," are divided into alphabetical listings of over 50,000 companies by product. So, if one had a perfect design for sunglasses, for example, one could look under "glasses: sun" and find a comprehensive listing of sunglass manufacturers.

Who Makes It and Where, Gayer-McAllister Publications, 51 Madison Avenue, New York, New York, 10010, (212) 689-4411; annual directory for stationery buyers and sellers.

Women's Wear Daily, published daily (except holidays and weekends) by Fairchild Publications, Inc., 7 East 12th Street, New York, NY 10003, (212) 741-6354. This is a newspaper, aimed at the garment industry. It carries listings of apparel and accessories shows, plus a classified section (jobs, services, business opportunities) that could provide leads.

In addition to pouring over trade magazines and annual directories, artists and designers who wish to add to their lists of contacts should peruse the glossy fashion and interior design magazines available at most newsstands and library reading rooms. Although these magazines are geared more toward the consumer than the merchandiser, they not only feature lush advertising spreads of various products (which could supply visual information as to the appropriateness of taking work to a particular manufacturer), they also provide manufacturer and supplier information about all the items pictured in editorial spreads on a specifically designated page. (For example, in **Vogue,** which is published monthly by Conde Naste Publications, Inc., Conde Naste Building, 350 Madison Avenue, New York, NY 10017, the page is called "In This Issue.")

Merchandise Markets

Many metropolitan centers have market centers, or merchandise marts, which are, in effect, permanent trade shows. The exhibitors display and sell their wares (wholesale) year-round. The goods are multyfold; including jewelry, clothes, furniture, etc. In most cases one can order a directory of the vendors in the market by calling the market's main office, or the director of the building. Here are the addresses and phone numbers for some of the markets in major cities.

Atlanta Merchandise Mart, 240 Peachtree Street, N.W., Atlanta, GA 30303, (404) 220-3000.

Dallas Trade Mart, 2100 Stemmons Freeway, Dallas, TX 75207 (214) 760-2852.

Los Angeles Merchandise Mart, 1933 South Broadway, Los Angeles, Ca 90014, (213) 749-7911.

Market Center, 230 Fifth Avenue, New York, NY 10010, (212) 532-4555.

The Merchandise Mart, Merchandise Plaza, Chicago, IL 60654, (312) 527-7600225 Fifth, 225 Fifth Avenue, New York, NY 10010, (212) 684-3200.

The Toy Building, 200 Fifth Avenue, New York, NY 10010 (212) 675-1141.

Western Merchandise Mart, 1355 Market Street, San Francisco, CA 94103, (415) 552-2311

Index

copyright, 14-15
requirement of, 40, 62
trademark, 23

P

Packaging, trademark protection
  for, 23
Patent and Trademark Office, 19
Patent notices, 40
Patents, 9, 11-12, 18-20
  infringement of, 20
  process of obtaining, 19
  term of, 19
  types of, 19
Plant Patents, 19
Production and related expenses, 69
Production schedule, 67-68
Product liability insurance, 56
Publications, 8, 106-9
Public domain works, 18
"purchase at cost" right, 59

Q

Quality control provisions, 47-49

R

Registration
  of copyrights, 16-17
  licensing agreement provision on,
    52-53
  of trademarks, 21-22, 53
Representations
  licensee's, 51-52
  licensor's, 38
Representatives. *See* Agents
Reservation of rights provision,
  38, 39
Royalties, 9
  advances against, 43-45
  basis of calculation of, 43
  comparative average, 105
  minimum, 43-45
  in model licensing agreement,
    41-45

nonrefundable, 43
rates, 42-43
when due, 43

S

Samples of licensed products, right
  to purchase, 59
Schedule A, 64-69
Schedule B, 70
Sell-off right, 58-59
Shows, licensing, 8
Sublicenses, 37-38
  provision on, 60-61
Submission form, 27

T

Termination of agreement, 56-58
Term of license, 64-66
Territory, 66-67
Trade dress, 23
Trademark Law Revision Act
  of 1988, 22
Trademarks, 9, 11-12, 20-23
  booklet on, 22
  clearance search, 22
  "intent to use" application, 22
  notices of, 23
  registration of, 21-22, 53

U

Unfair competition, 27
Unsold inventory, 59
Useful articles, copyrights not
  available for, 13
Utility patents, 19

W

Waiver form, 27
Waiver provision, 61
Warranty, licensor's, 38-39
Works made for hire, 17
Written agreement, need for a, 9-10